David Palmer

BUSINESS ASSIGNMENTS

• VIDEO ACTIVITY BOOK •

Based on original case studies
by Ken Casler & David Palmer

Oxford University Press

Oxford University Press, Great Clarendon Street, Oxford, OX2 6DP

Oxford New York
Athens Auckland Bangkok Bogota Bombay Buenos Aires
Calcutta Cape Town Dar es Salaam Delhi Florence Hong Kong
Istanbul Karachi Kuala Lumpur Madras Madrid Melbourne
Mexico City Nairobi Paris Singapore Taipei Tokyo Toronto Warsaw

and associated companies in
Berlin Ibadan

OXFORD and OXFORD ENGLISH
are trade marks of Oxford University Press

First published 1993
Second impression 1997

ISBN 0 19 458353 8 (Video Activity Book)
ISBN 0 19 458049 0 (Video Guide)

ISBN 0 19 458335 X (VHS PAL Video Cassette 1)
ISBN 0 19 458344 9 (VHS PAL Video Cassette 2)
ISBN 0 19 458336 8 (VHS SECAM Video Cassette 1)
ISBN 0 19 458345 7 (VHS SECAM Video Cassette 2)
ISBN 0 19 458337 6 (VHS NTSC Video Cassette 1)
ISBN 0 19 458346 5 (VHS NTSC Video Cassette 2)
ISBN 0 19 458338 4 (BETAMAX PAL Video Cassette 1)
ISBN 0 19 458347 3 (BETAMAX PAL Video Cassette 2)
ISBN 0 19 458339 2 (BETAMAX SECAM Video Cassette 1)
ISBN 0 19 458348 1 (BETAMAX SECAM Video Cassette 2)
ISBN 0 19 458340 6 (BETAMAX NTSC Video Cassette 1)
ISBN 0 19 458349 X (BETAMAX NTSC Video Cassette 2)

© David Palmer, 1993

Printed in Malta by Interprint.

Acknowledgements:
Oxford Illustrators, Pete Lawrence – Oxprint.
Stills photography by Rob Judges. Cover photography by Martyn Chillmaid.

The publisher and author would like to thank the following for their help and
advice in publishing these materials:
Colchester English Study Centre, Colchester.
IFG LANGUES, Paris La defense.
Language Centre, Manchester Business School, Manchester.
Linguarama, Box, Wiltshire.
Regent Language Training Ltd, London.
York Associates, Paris.

There might be instances where we have been unable to trace or contact the copyright
holder before our printing deadline. We apologize for this apparent negligence. If notified,
the publisher will be pleased to rectify any errors or omissions at the earliest opportunity.

IPSA Industries

GROUNDWORK

Phase One

1.1 Using your own experience, note down the advantages and disadvantages of exclusive agency agreements, either from the point of view of the company or the distributor.

1.2 Discussion Discuss your points in groups.

Phase Two

2.1 ▶ Watch the opening sequence of the video up to the beginning of scene 1. Which part of the world are we in? What city is this?

Now read through all the activities in Phase Two.

▶ Watch scenes 1 and 2, up to the moment when one man leaves the restaurant.

2.2 Complete the landing card for character A.

REPUBLIC OF INDONESIA	Disembarkation/ Embarkation Card	Official use only ☐☐☐☐☐☐	RIU-637399 D

Full name (write surname first, use block letters)		Sex
		1 ☐ male 2 ☐ female

Nationality	Profession	First trip to Indonesia?
		1 ☐ Yes 2 ☐ No

Company name	Nature of business	

Purpose of visit	Accommodation	Date of arrival
1 ☐ Business 3 ☐ Education	1 ☐ Hotel 3 ☐ Residence of friend/relative	
2 ☐ Holiday 4 ☐ Other	2 ☐ Apartment 4 ☐ Other	/ /

2.3 Complete the business card order for character B.

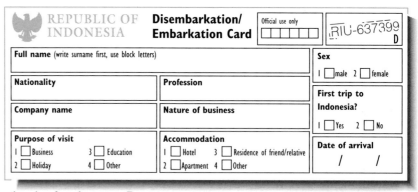

In the spaces provided enter the text as you wish it to appear on the card.
(1) Full Name
(2) Title/job function *
(3) Name of Company #
(4) Address of Company *
(5) Business of Company *
(6) Telephone and
(7) Fax Numbers
* Please select required typeface from our catalogue quoting reference.
\# Please supply artwork/bromide for logo, if required, and attach it to your order.

(1) ....
(2) *General Manager* ....
(3) ....
(4) *P.O. Box J. KST., 3rd Floor,* .....
     Jalan M.H. Thamrin No. 51, ..
     Djakarta, Indonesia ....
(5) ....
(6) *44.326.403* (7) *44.326.803* ......

2.4 Complete this letter from character C, to B, introducing A.

<u>**Argyle Taylor Bank Plc**</u>
Yman Bonjol 77, Djakarta, Republic of Indonesia   *Tel 333789 Fax 333792*

. . . .
General Manager
. . . . Company
PO Box JKST
3rd Floor, Jalan M H Thamrin No.51
. . . .

12 May 1988

Dear . . . .
       Just a line to confirm the arrangements for tomorrow night at the
Intercontinental.
       I shall be bringing along . . . . of . . . .
. . . . He is keen on setting up a . . . . in . . . . for
his company's . . . . equipment, which has been successfully exported
worldwide and done particularly well in tropical markets.
       I should like to assure you that Argyle Taylor has full confidence in Ipsa as
a well-established and reliable trading partner. I would urge you to consider
carefully what they have to offer before making a decision concerning . . . .,
who you say have already approached you.
       I look forward to our meeting.
Yours sincerely,

. . . . South East Asia Area Manager

Phase Three

3.1 What difficulties do you predict for Webster? Make a list.

NUTS & BOLTS

Phase One

1.1 Vocabulary building ▶ Watch scene 1 of the video again and write in column 2 the words or phrases that have the same meaning as those definitions listed in column 1.

1 DEFINITION	**2** WORD OR PHRASE USED IN VIDEO
visit	
sales literature	
reserving (a hotel room)	
interested in getting	
arranged	
very important and essential	
field of business	
understand	
(I) agree entirely	
products	

Phase Two

2.1 Brainstorm With your colleagues brainstorm a list of general questions you would want to ask a potential distributor of Ipsa's products in a new market.

2.2 ▶ Now watch the rest of scene 2 and complete Webster's questions below.

What are … ?	*What about … ?*	*Do you see … ?*
How do … ?	*I suppose … ?*	*Do you do … ?*
What's the … ?	*I would guess … ?*	*Are we … ?*
What are … ?	*What are … ?*	*And what about … ?*
Any … ?		

Which of your questions were asked? Note any differences in the language used.

Why does Webster use the question forms: *I suppose … ? I would guess … ?*

2.3 The wrong end of the stick It is easy to be misinformed. Correct the following statements.

Indonesia has a first class network of road communications.

To deal with a complex market like this, you need to have good Indonesian office workers.

Recent developments mean that there is no future for forestry equipment sales in Indonesia.

Sujarwo rely entirely on government contracts.

Sujarwo are well established in the chainsaw business.

Sujarwo's customers like to arrange for maintenance themselves.

The Indonesian Government does not allow the import of spare parts.

Phase Three

3.1 Before visiting Banes at his office in Djakarta, Webster made some notes on the key advantages of Ipsa over Bleckenbauer.

▶ Watch scene 3 of the video to reconstruct these notes.

> • products better suited ....
> • products require ....
> • distributors and operators ....
> ....
> • Ipsa's fastest growing ....
> ....
> • Ipsa have equipment working in ....
> .... which have ....
>
> Notes

3.2 What are Banes's objections to Ipsa? How does Webster answer these objections?

FOLLOW UP

Phase One

1.1 Phoning home Webster called head office from his hotel to report on his progress. Role-play part of this call.

Role 1:
MANAGING DIRECTOR, IPSA
Using the question forms you studied in Nuts & Bolts 2.1 and 2.2, prepare to ask Webster about the competition in Indonesia, the essential requirements for selling Ipsa's products there, and the chances of success.

Role 2:
PAUL WEBSTER,
EXPORT DIRECTOR, IPSA
Report back on the competition, and market requirements using the rough notes below that Webster made at his meeting with Banes.

Notes

gd contacts Min Forestry essential + gvt contracts,
but private mills impt.
Banes now handles different prodcts but no prob if –
essential pts • gd maintenance + service bkup
• not contractors
• guarantee pts & service
competition • imports most impt
• local mfrs – on increase encouraged by gvt
• japs – price
• Bleckenbauer – exclusivity

Phase Two

2.1 Mini presentation Make a presentation to convince Banes's partner, Adnan Basiroen, of the superiority of Ipsa's products over those of the competition.

Design an OHP slide or flipchart presentation using information from the video.

Using your visual(s) make a short oral presentation to your colleagues.

Note: Concentrate on the following aspects of making a presentation.

♦ Tell your audience what you are going to say.

♦ Say it.

♦ Tell them what you have said.

♦ Maintain eye contact with your audience, or focus on their noses.

♦ Make sure both of your feet are firmly on the ground, and keep your hands around waist level, avoiding dramatic gestures.

♦ Never criticise the competition.

Make your presentation. Then evaluate your colleagues' presentations on a scale of 1-5 (maximum) according to the following criteria:

• simplicity and clarity of visuals
• eye contact

• clarity of verbal message
• poise

PAY OFF

Phase One

1.1 Green issues Classify the following terms in some way and then explain your classification.

ozone friendly	phosphate free	organically produced
acid rain	environmentally friendly	greenhouse effect
unleaded petrol	deforrestation	toxic waste
safe alternatives	ozone layer	recycling

1.2 Which of the terms concern Ipsa? Do any of the terms concern your company?

1.3 Choose one of the terms and prepare to talk about it for two minutes.

Phase Two

2.1 'Green capitalists'

'Many companies have begun to see the environmental issue as a selling advantage, as a reason for buying their product rather than the competitor's.'
Source: ***International Management***

Choose one of the following products, or talk about your company's products:

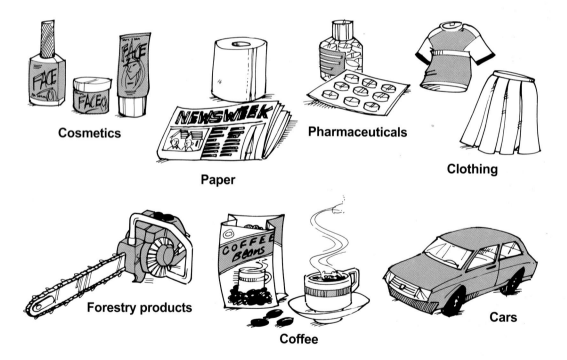

Cosmetics

Paper

Pharmaceuticals

Clothing

Forestry products

Coffee

Cars

How could any of the issues discussed above be used as a selling advantage for this product? Give some examples of companies that are doing this.

For the product you have chosen, design a newspaper advertisement, television commercial, press release, or mission statement using environmental issues to the advantage of the company.

AUDIT

Checklist

to drop in = to visit informally, without an appointment
> e.g. *We dropped in on some friends.*

to sort out = to put something into order
> e.g. *The secretary sorts out the mail before opening it.*
> INFORMALLY - to arrange, to solve (a problem)
> e.g. *Can we sort out a date for that meeting?*

to be after something = to try to get something
> e.g. *I'm after your account.* = I hope to get your account.
> *He's after his boss's job.*

Fire away (invariable) **=** Start asking questions. Go ahead with your interrogation.

a shake-out (n) (colloquial) = a very extensive reorganization
> e.g. *There's been a big shake-out in the whole timber business.*

in the *main*/the *main* thing = generally, usually/ the most important thing
> e.g. *In the main there's no choice but to buy foreign products.*
> *The main thing is our customers won't sign an order without a guarantee.*

cutting away the dead wood (metaphor) = removing useless or unproductive elements
(in this case unprofitable businesses)

a knotty problem = a difficult or complex problem

Phrase bank

BUSINESS:	SOCIAL:
track record	My pleasure.
manufacturing base	Don't mention it.
a key person	See you.
a joint venture	Sure you won't have another drink?
a contractor	
added value	GENERAL:
in the field	stuff (informal)
top-level contacts	bumf (informal)
facts and figures	sizeable (adj)
to push a deal through	crucial (adj)
we haven't got money to throw away	pretty fast, pretty rough (colloquial)
	to be keen on someone/something
	to be bound to do something

Main focus

Questioning statements Sometimes it is easier to make conversation by asking questions less directly. Webster uses statements as questions in his conversation with Banes. Notice his intonation.

I suppose it's worthwhile having good contacts there?

I would guess that you rely a lot on government contracts?

Cougar Japan

GROUNDWORK

Phase One

1.1 Consultation The following companies have consulted you about extending their product range under these brand names. You should recommend either **related diversification** (different products related to the company's basic product) or **horizontal diversification** (other versions/models of the same product). First consider whether people associate the brand name closely with a specific product or more with a brand image which could be used to sell closely, or even distantly related products. Suggest suitable products for diversification.

COMPANY/BRAND NAME	ASSOCIATED WITH PRODUCT IMAGE	RECOMMENDED DIVERSIFICATION		SUGGESTED PRODUCTS
		HORIZONTAL	RELATED	
Marks & Spencer				
Kodak				
Sony				
BP				
Perrier				
Ricoh				
KLM				
Norwich Union				
Your Company				

Phase Two

2.1 ▶ Watch scene 1 of the video and scene 2 up to when the Japanese person is introduced. Try and complete the company organization chart below:

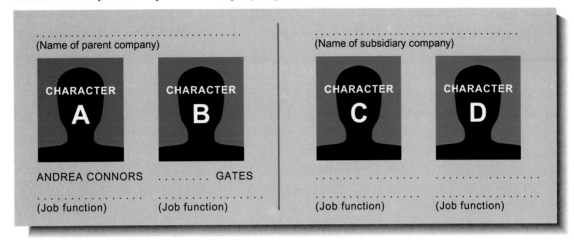

2.2 Which of these photographs represents characters A,B,C and D? Write in their names.

Phase Three

3.1 Delete as necessary to form correct statements.

Nicholson/Gates/Connors is visiting Korea/Japan next week.

Nicholson/Gates/Connors is recommending diversifying into clothes in Europe/Japan.

Nicholson/Gates/Connors is recommending going down market with shoes in Japan/Europe.

Diversifying into clothes/extending the shoe range down market is official company strategy for Cougar International.

Nicholson/Gates/Connors thinks that it is too soon/late to diversify into clothes/extend the shoe range down market in Japan.

Nicholson/Gates/Connors feels sure that Cougar should promote its image of quality in Japan by diversifying into clothes/extending the shoe range down market.

Nicholson/Gates/Connors is open-minded about group strategy.

NUTS & BOLTS

Phase One

1.1 **Silent viewing** You are going to see a flipchart presentation of Cougar Japan's alternative marketing plan. The flip chart frames used in this presentation are shown at the top of page 12.

COUGAR JAPAN **MARKETING STRATEGIES** FULL LINE DISTIBUTION / PRODUCT DIVERSIFICATION HIGH-GRADE SPORTS SHOES / HIGH-GRADE SPORTS CLOTHES ↓ MEDIUM-PRICE SPORTS SHOES ↓ LOW-PRICE SPORTS SHOES	*"WHY GO DOWNMARKET NOW?" *"WHY **NOT** DIVERSIFY NOW?"	"WHY GO DOWNMARKET NOW?" * The Japanese market is strikingly similar to other Cougar International markets.	* Middle and lower market segments offer unique opportunities in the current climate.	*"WHY **NOT** DIVERSIFY NOW?" * Japanese distributors want guarantees that a product range will be supported over the long term. * This guarantee is best provided by demonstrating ability to capture ever larger market shares.
FRAME 1 Language notes:	**FRAME 2** Language notes:	**FRAME 3** Language notes:	**FRAME 4** Language notes:	**FRAME 5** Language notes:
Body language notes:	Body language notes:	Body language notes:	Body language notes:	Body language notes:

▶ Watch scene 2, the presentation, ***without the sound***.

Note down below each frame words, phrases and expressions which you think Saito is using. Include the expressions he will need to introduce each frame.

Observe Gates. What do you think his reaction is? How does his body language and that of the other men show this?

1.2 Using your notes, make a short presentation of these frames to your colleague(s).

1.3 ▶ Now watch the sequence again ***with the sound***, and note:

♦ Important differences between your presentation and Saito's.

♦ How the body language matched the verbal language used. Can you suggest any reasons for the contrast between Gates's body language and that of Nicholson and Saito?

Phase Two

2.1 Making a point ▶ Watch scene 4. Note the language used by Gates and Nicholson to make the following points in their argument:

POINT MADE	LANGUAGE USED TO MAKE IT
Gates	
Our future's with sports clothes.	. . . .
I don't think your proposal's feasible.	. . . .
It's my responsibility.	. . . .
You'll confuse the customer.	. . . .
Now we should diversify.	. . . .

Nicholson

We should build on the success we have. . . . .

Japan is not like Europe. . . . .

Japan is a complex market. . . . .

We need market share. . . . .

It would be dangerous to change strategy. . . . .

It won't work.

FOLLOW UP

Phase One

1.1 Vocabulary building Match the words in columns 1 and 2 to make expressions used in the video. Then match them with their meanings in column 3.

1	2	3
a real	posted	you can't hide the fact that
keep me	alley	a dead end
full-line	disguising	an annoying person
there's no	pain	considered with care
viewed with	ball game	have any possibility of success
proven	ability	an excellent chance
a golden	distributor	let me know what's happening
a different	opportunity	a successful track record
a blind	caution	another kind of problem
stand	a chance	a trader handling a complete product range

Phase Two

2.1 Role-play preparation Using the transcript, prepare a flipchart or overhead presentation of Gate's (or your own) strategy for Japan. First make notes under the following headings:

GROUP STRATEGY

MARKET IMAGE

THE JAPANESE MARKET

PROPOSAL FOR DIVERSIFICATION IN JAPAN

DISRIBUTORS

COMPETITION

Then prepare your flipchart or overhead frames. Make sure the visuals are simple. You will expand on the points in your verbal presentation.

2.2 Look again at Phase Two of **NUTS & BOLTS** and study the points made by Nicholson and the language used to make them.

2.3 Role-play the presentation. Those watching the presentation should argue against the proposals.

Phase Three

3.1 Complete this section on Japanese distributors from a country brief on Japan in **The Far East Business Conspectus**.

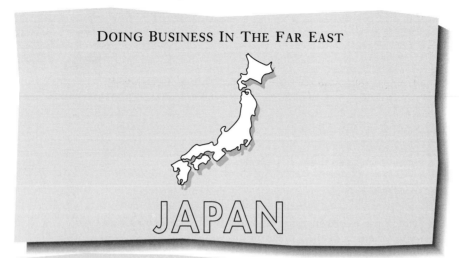

DOING BUSINESS IN THE FAR EAST

JAPAN

DISTRIBUTION

The Japanese distribution system . . . . relatively complex compared with other . . . . Distributors prefer or even require . . . . to commit themselves over a . . . . term. Distributors are mistrustful of . . . . whose product lines change or . . . . unobtainable at short notice.

    Distributors . . . . reassured when a supplier shows . . . . his objective is to . . . . market share over a sustained . . . .

PAY OFF

Phase One

1.1 Mini case study The following incident occurred at a Japanese car plant in Britain:

> *'Two drums stood together, for fire-safety reasons, in the same part of the plant. An employee connected the wrong drum to a pump, so that bottles awaiting windscreen washing liquid were filled with the wrong fluid. This went on for some time before the mistake was discovered. A lot of bottles had to be drained, washed out and refilled, wasting time and money.'*
> Source: **The Director**

As a manager, what action would you take as a result of this incident?

If a similar incident happened in your own company, what action would be taken?

Propose your solutions to your colleagues and agree on the best one.

What action do you think the Japanese company took?

Phase Two

2.1 Preparation for discussion

> *'When a contract says three per cent rejects are accepted, the supplier sends 97 per cent good ones and thinks that's all right, that meets the contract. But the Japanese mentality, even though three per cent is in the contract, is to strive to make it zero.'*
> Source: ***The Director***

East and West Which of the following working practices/business attitudes/ management techniques are particularly Japanese, and which more Western. Which would be accepted in your country? Which would you like to adopt in your company and why? Complete the matrix with a plus (+) or minus (-) as appropriate.

	JAPAN	WEST	ACCEPTABLE	I WOULD ADOPT
It is common for a foreigner to be on the board of directors.				
Management and other staff eat in the same company canteen.				
The company tries to involve wives and families by inviting them to social events.				
Management have reserved parking spaces.				
Male colleagues expect to socialize together every evening after work, before returning to their wives.				
All members of the company wear the same overalls including the MD.				
Every employee has a detailed job description.				
Employees do not lose money if they are late or absent.				
Being aggressive is considered essential for success in the competitive world of business.				
At the beginning of the day staff sing the company song together.				
Individual initiative and achievement are rewarded.				
Meetings are used to debate problems and take important decisions.				
People who work late are highly regarded.				
Age and seniority are respected.				
Most decisions are made by senior management.				

2.2 Compare and discuss your results with your colleagues.

AUDIT

Checklist

to bring someone round to an idea/proposal
= to convince or persuade someone that the idea or proposal is right

to come out with
= to invent, to express
e.g. *Nicholson's always coming out with wild schemes.*
= Nicholson is always proposing unusual (and unacceptable) ideas.

(not) to pull punches (metaphor usually used in negative) = not to hide the truth
e.g. *I'm not going to pull any punches.*

It grows on you (metaphor) = You gradually begin to like it.

to stick one's neck out (metaphor) = to take risks

to be up to something = to be doing something suspicious

tried and tested (collocation) = tested very fully and proven to be successful

the key to *success/fame/market share* (metaphor) = the best way to obtain

Phrase bank

BUSINESS:	SOCIAL:
market segments	I don't believe you two have met before.
a clothing venture	Cheers!
a slice of the market	
a full-line distributor	**GENERAL:**
a long-term committment	kids (informal)
a lower price range	the near future
market image	feasible (adj)
established group stategy	to convince/to be convinced
to diversify	to stop over in (place)
to go up/down market	to be no point in doing something
to do one's homework	to back someone/something up
	to have the potential
	to have someone/something in mind
	to go into detail

Main focus

Interrupting

This is all very interesting, but I don't see …

Look, I hate to interrupt (but) …

Hang on …

Dealing with interruptions

Point taken.

I would agree with your arguments, but I would add …

Chocolats Memlinck

GROUNDWORK

Phase One

1.1 **Quality and tradition** Note down three products that have an image of quality and tradition. How is this image promoted?

PRODUCT	PROMOTIONAL STRATEGIES
1	
2	
3	

1.2 These two lists are the ingredients of two different brands of filled chocolates. Study them carefully.

The lists show basic ingredients and additives.

Contrast the basic ingredients.

> *plain chocolate 40% cocoa solids with emulsifier: E322, modified starch, flavourings, gelling agent: E440, fat-reduced cocoa, salt, acidity regulators: E331 and E330, dried egg white, emulsifier: E471, molasses, colours: E160a, E127 and cochineal*

> Sugar, Hazelnuts
> Full cream milk powder
> Cocoa butter, Cocoa paste
> Emulsifier: lecithin
> Flavour: vanillin
>
> Plain chocolate minimum 60%
> Cocoa solids

What is the function of the various additives?

    gelling agent   emulsifier   flavouring

How does this affect the marketing and promotion of the product? Consider:

    PRICING   UNIQUE SELLING POINTS   MARKET IMAGE

    PACKAGING   PACKING   DISTRIBUTION

Phase Two

2.1 ▶ Watch scene 1 (up to the point where Paul tastes the last chocolate).

Who do you think the two characters are and what is their relationship?

Why is Paul tasting the chocolates?

2.2 ▶ Watch this sequence again and complete the Description and Tasting remarks columns in the test chart on page 18.

2.3 Suggest some reasons for Paul's tasting remarks.

Chocolats Memlinck S.A.

TASTE REPORT

Tasting sequence	Description 1 Coating 2 Filling	Brand	Tasting Remarks	Comments/action
1	1 milk			
	2 praline	Old Masters		
2	1 almond			
	2 cream			
3	1			
	2 marzipan			
4	1			
	2 coffee truffle	Charleston Collection.		

2.4 ▶ Watch more of scene 1, up to the point where Eileen says: ... *a few concessions to their taste?* Complete as much of the chart as possible.

2.5 Prediction What do you think Paul's reaction will be? What issues will he wish to discuss?

NUTS & BOLTS

Phase One

1.1 ▶ Continue to watch scene 1, up to the point where Eileen says: ... *we're going to have to talk about price first.* Complete this New Product Record card.

Wessner's **GOURMET FOODS INC.** 1133 Lexington Ave. Boston Mass. 02172

NEW PRODUCT RECORD (continuation)

Product name: Belgian filled chocolates Supplier: Chocolats Memlinck SA, Ave. Franklin Roosevelt, 107 1000, Brussels, Belgium. Contact: Paul Van Houton

Date week ending	Average purchases per week	Average wt/units per custr.	Store traffic per week	Retail price per lb $
26.04.86	57.9	. . . .	. . . .	25.20
03.05.86	58.3	. . . .	. . . .	25.20
10.05.86	59.7	. . . .	. . . .	25.20
17.05.86	. . . .	. . . .	. . . .	25.20

Phase Two

2.1 Hand Signals How do you use your hands to express yourself? ▶ Watch the rest of scene 1 *without the sound*. Observe the hand gestures made by Paul and Eileen. The phrases in column 1 show what they might be saying with each gesture. Indicate which phrases match Paul's gestures and which match Eileen's by putting **P** and **E** in the appropriate boxes.

1		2
a)	*I understand what you are saying, but ...*	
b)	*If you will excuse me ...*	
c)	*I can't do anything about prices ...*	
d)	*I apologise, but ...*	
e)	*That is just not reasonable!*	
f)	*That goes against what you said before.*	
g)	*If you agree, we have a bargain.*	
h)	*OK, but you would have to accept ...*	

2.2 ▶ Now watch the sequence *with the sound* and note in column 2 the actual words used with the gestures.

Phase Three

3.1 Positive talk When it is in the interests of both parties to come to an agreement in a negotiation, it is important to keep the discussions moving by using positive language.

▶ Watch the video again from after the tasting to where Eileen says: *I'm going to need stable prices*. Raise your hand whenever Eileen or Paul makes a positive statement. Note the actual words used.

3.2 Listed below are a number of points made by Eileen in her negotiations with Paul.
▶ Watch the video to:

Complete the points (a - g).

Link them with the issues: PRICE, SHELF LIFE, MARKET PREFERENCE.

POINT	ISSUE	RESPONSE
a) *In my . . . . . . we have to find an . . . . . . way to make the product . . . .*		☐
b) *Americans . . . . . . prefer their chocolates . . . . . . and . . . .*		☐
c) *We could try and do a . . . . . . for special . . . . . . but it pushes up . . . .*		☐
d) *A . . . . like fresh chocolate . . . . . . high . . . . . . and . . . . insurance costs.*		☐
e) *There are plenty of very . . . . products in there too.*		☐
f) *With the . . . . like crazy we could . . . . losing . . . . . . per cent of our . . . . . . !*		☐
g) *We'd also like to . . . . . . on . . . .*		☐

3.3 Now mark in Paul's response to each point in the chart above.

1 *I realize it isn't easy.*

2 *There's a price rise in the pipeline.*

3 *Tradition is our selling point.*

4 *I'd need a letter of credit. It's company policy.*

5 *There must be a way round this problem.*

6 *It could send our costs too high.*

7 *I'd hate to see our prospects in the US ruined by overpricing.*

FOLLOW UP

Phase One

1.1 Vocabulary building The words on page 20 are all taken from the video and will be useful to you in Phases Two and Three. In what context would you expect to find them used? Group the words under the appropriate headings below. Be prepared to give an example of each word used in the context you have selected.

Some words may fit in several contexts.

shelf life	aftertaste	carton	consignment	open account
batch	to bump up	sensitive	operation	stagger
set up	unit	truckline	leeway	letter of credit
absorb	ultimatum	discount	pass on	concession
perishable	overpricing	freeze	middle ground	

DISTRIBUTION	PRICING	COSTS	TERMS OF TRADE	NEGOTIATIONS

Phase Two

2.1 The chart below summarizes the issues and arguments raised in the Memlinck negotiations. Part of the chart has been completed as an example. Try to complete the rest from your knowledge of the case.

ISSUE	PROBLEM	SOLUTION PROPOSED BY EILEEN	PAUL'S COUNTER ARGUMENT
MARKET PREFERENCE			
SHELF LIFE	Chocolates are going sour if held up during distribution.	Add very small amounts of natural preservative to increase shelf life to 31 days.	Additives affect the taste of the chocolates and destroy the traditional image of Memlinck. Memlinck can only compete with American style products if it keeps its traditional image.
PRICE			
TERMS OF TRADE			

2.2 Now check your chart from the transcript or by watching the video again.

Phase Three

3.1 **Role-play** Prepare to role-play a negotiation about the problems summarized in Phase Two. Approach the issues *either* from the point of view of Eileen, *or* Paul. Before starting the negotiation, are there any other solutions you can propose for each problem? Are there any solutions you are definitely not prepared to accept?

3.2 Now role-play the discussions. Try to keep the negotiations moving by using some of the positive language you studied in NUTS & BOLTS, but be firm and do not accept any solutions that would be against your company's interests.

PAY OFF

Phase One

1.1 What do the following have in common?

1.2

> '*Consider the case of Richard Cooper, who accidentally struck a pedestrian while bicycling in New York's Central Park. Cooper and the pedestrian, a Weight Watchers International lawyer became friends. This relationship led to Cooper quitting his job and buying the Chicago franchise for Weight Watchers. By age twenty-nine, Richard Cooper was a millionaire.*'
> Source: **Contemporary Business by Boone and Kurtz**

Which business franchises have been successful in your country? Do they share any common characteristics?

1.3 Work with your colleagues. Summarize *either* the advantages *or* the disadvantages of becoming a franchisee.

Phase Two

2.1 **Role-play** A number of retail franchises specializing in Belgian chocolates are operating successfully internationally. Chocolats Memlinck are interested in franchising the retail of their own products and have organized an informal presentation and information meeting to discuss possibilities. The meeting is between **Franchisors** representing Chocolats Memlinck, and **Franchisees** representing potential purchasers of the franchises. Prepare for the meeting with the help of the briefing notes below:

FRANCHISORS Your objective is to present the attractions of your franchise to potential franchisees. Although this is only an informal meeting to sound out the interest, you should be prepared with your general ideas on the following points. If necessary prepare visuals to help your presentation.

- products and image
- support given to the franchisee
- market, territory, exclusivity
- length of contract, renewal, termination, resale terms
- what kind of person you are looking for to be a franchisee
- what the franchise package will consist of
- training
- fees and investment

Note: Substitute another product of your choice if you prefer.

FRANCHISEES Although franchises are amongst the most successful small businesses, you are advised to be very sceptical. Find out as much as possible about the Franchisor and his package. Prepare especially questions about the following points:

- start up investment and financing
- restrictions and controls by the franchisor
- length of agreement, termination and renewal
- training
- the competition
- promotional and other support
- opening
- premises
- purchase of stock
- exclusivity and territory
- renewal of equipment

2.2 Franchisors and Franchisees meet. Franchisors make a brief presentation of your franchise package and then take questions from the Franchisees.

AUDIT

Checklist

a bug (n) (colloquial) = something that is preventing a system or machine from operating effectively.
e.g. *a bug in a computer programme*

an unqualified success = a complete success. Often used in the negative.
e.g. *I would not call it an unqualified success.*

leeway (n. noncount) = Literally: the sideways movement of a ship caused by wind. Metaphorically: space for manoeuvre or possibility for changing an arrangement.
e.g. *I don't have any leeway on prices.* = I have no opportunity to change prices.

to crack an issue = to solve a problem
e.g. *We have to crack the issue of shelf life* = We have to solve the problem of shelf life.

to boil down to (metaphor) = to reduce from a complex or multiple issue to a simple or single issue.
e.g. *What it boils down to is costs.* = The basic problem is costs.

to bump up (colloquial) = to increase
e.g. *We bumped up the shelf life by using additives.*

on that front (metaphor) = in that problem area. Cf. on the price front, on the distribution front = concerning the problem of prices, distribution, etc.

a little on the sour side = slightly sour. Cf. These trousers are on the large side.
= These trousers are slightly too large for me.

Phrase bank

BUSINESS:		GENERAL:
a perishable import	beyond its shelf life	a remedy (n)
a discount	We have a deal	minute (adj)
a letter of credit	to get off the ground	adequate (adj)
a mark up		decent (adj)
a foothold	SOCIAL:	
a price freeze		in the pipeline
a batch	I'm afraid I did	on our hands
a selling point	I see what you're getting at	
customer reaction	I thought that's what you'd say	to cope with someone/something
unit costs	Hold on!	to stagger
price sensitive	I hear you	to absorb
	I grant you that	

Main focus

Keeping negotiations open

There must be a way round this problem.

There must be some middle ground.

I realize it isn't easy.

HAL Information Systems

GROUNDWORK

Phase One

1.1 Blind Listening Listen to the first two speakers in scene 1 up to where the man says ... *no end.*

What are they doing?

What are they talking about?

What can you predict about this case?

1.2 What aspects of your work, or your department's work, are done by computers? How effectively are they handled? Make brief notes on the outline below. Then explain to your colleagues the problems or limitations of your information technology facilities, and how they could be improved or upgraded.

	COMPUTER USED FOR:	PROBLEMS/LIMITATIONS	SUGGESTIONS FOR IMPROVEMENT/UPGRADING
1			
2			
3			

Phase Two

2.1 Mime Listen to the soundtrack of scenes 1, 2 and 3 without watching the image.

While you are listening, make notes on the scenes and characters:

- ♦ Where does the action take place? (Describe any objects, furniture, etc. you think will appear.)

- ♦ What are the characters doing? (Are they standing/sitting?)

- ♦ What is the expression on their faces as they speak?

- ♦ Try to guess also the ages of the characters and say something about their personalities and their professional status in the company.

2.2 When you and your colleagues are ready, play the soundtrack again and mime the action as realistically as possible.

2.3 Now ▶ watch the video up to the end of scene 3 and compare it with your own version.

NUTS & BOLTS

Phase One

1.1 Try and complete this telephone conversation.

Thomas: *Hello, Mr Gray?*

Gray: *Yes.*

Thomas: . . . . , *we seem to have* . . . . . .

. . . .

Gray: *Not again! We may be just another customer to you, but without those parts we*

can't look after our own customers . . . .

. . . . , *surely.*

Thomas: *I know, Mr Gray.* . . . .

. . . .

Gray: *I thought* . . . .

. . . . *Look, either* . . . .

. . . . , *or we'll have to* . . . . *Goodbye!*

▶ Watch scene 2 again and compare it with your version.

1.2 Role-play ▶ Watch scene 3 again and then with a colleague act out this telephone conversation between Clare Thomas and Alan Newman.

Clare Thomas

Alan Newman

Ask Alan if he's free to talk about a problem

Explain why you are not free, and ask if it's urgent

Briefly describe what has happened with Gray

Express concern – Gray is one of Slater's best accounts

Give a brief summary of the computer problem you would like to talk to Alan about

Be sceptical, but arrange to meet. Tell Clare what information you will need at the meeting

Acknowledge and close the conversation

Phase Two

2.1 Below is a letter Ken Jenkins wrote to Alan Newman, following up his product
demonstration. ▶ Watch scene 4 to complete the letter. There is one dot per letter.

HAL
INFORMATION SYSTEMS

HAL Information Systems PLC
12 Chiltern Lane   Century Business Park   Reading   Berks RG9 2DT
Tel. (0628) 734756   Fax (0628) 745767   Telex 45989 HAL

Mr Alan Newman
Slater Engineering Plc
243 Birmingham Road, Walsall
WS5 3AA

31 July 1989

Dear Mr Newman,

    I was very glad to meet you last week and to have the chance of
demonstrating the HAL . . . local . . . . system. I am writing
to put on paper the . . . . I described during our meeting
and to confirm the rough price . . . . I gave you then.

    The key advantages of the HAL . . . system for Slater Engineering
would be as follows:

- The HAL . . . . area . . . . will allow full
  . n . . . . n of data, allowing order processing to be fully
  integrated with stock control. You simply put in the relevant
  information, for example, ... a . . . . y, or . . . . . .
  . . . .

- The HAL . . . offers full multi-user capability, allowing
  several . . . to be linked up with a . . . . to
  . . . . . data at the same time.

- F . . . . can be converted from your . . . . computer
  system to the HAL . . . . Furthermore, because the HAL . . . uses
  the same . . . . as the PC you have got now, it
  will work with your current system.

- All the PCs in the system are c . . . . by c . . . . so
  they can c . . . . with . . . .

- The system is simple to upgrade, allowing . . c . . . . such
  as . . . . o . . . . and . . s . . . . . . t . . . .

    The overall price of £ . . . . . would be a realistic figure
to cover:

- 1 HAL . . . central disc server   • 5 PCs with full colour VDUs
- 5 daisywheel printers   • Software packages, including Communications
Manager, Accounts Manager, Database Manager and Word Manager
- Installation and maintenance

    This estimate is based on the description of your needs you
supplied to me last week. I should greatly value, however, the chance
to visit Slater's, to see at first-hand the specific problems you
have encountered, and talk in more detail about the different
financial arrangements we offer.

    Could I get in touch early next week to suggest a time when
we might meet again?

       Yours sincerely,

K. Jenkins

Ken Jenkins, Technical Sales Representative

2.2 The following numbers are all used in the video. Note down what they refer to.

NUMBER	REFERS TO		NUMBER	REFERS TO
900			50,000	
>1,400			19	
4098			8,000	
twice			4 minimum	
4				

2.3 With a colleague practice asking questions that will elicit the numbers listed in **2.2** above.

FOLLOW UP

Phase One

1.1 **Vocabulary building** Match the words in column 1 with the appropriate words in column 2 to form collocations used in the video. More collocations can be formed by using words from 3 either before or after the words in 1 and 2.

1	2	3	
compatible	estimate	scanner	symbol
active	file	card	discontinued
credit	system	department	beam
basic	range	free	sketch
product	availability	costs	manager
electronic	software	partners	limit
rough	printing	limited	integrated
unit	mail	black	box
master	status	low	offset
operating	accounts	full	quarterly
laser	lines		

Phase Two

2.1 **Keeping the customer satisfied** Look again at the telephone conversation between Gray and Thomas in NUTS & BOLTS **1.1** Gray has had problems at Slater's before. With a colleague prepare and role-play the telephone conversation between Gray and Thomas the first time this happened.

GRAY You have ordered replacement filters for your vehicle washing machine, but these have not been delivered yet, although you received the invoice for them by return. Slater's are usually quite efficient and this is the first delivery problem you have experienced with them.

THOMAS Gray is one of your oldest customers. You do not wish to upset him. You have already had problems like this with other customers, but never before with Gray. Do everything you can to reassure Gray.

Note: If you prefer, role-play a conversation with one of your own company's customers concerning a problem caused by your company's computer.

Phase Three

3.1 [▶] Watch scene 4 again or check the transcript to find phrases with a similar meaning to the following:

In future you could improve your system with add-on components.

= . . . .

You would be economizing in as much as you can retain your present software.

= . . . .

All that's necessary is to centralize the information.

= . . . .

OK, but aren't we simply paying more for more or less identical capability?

= . . . .

It'll be cheaper in the long-term.

= . . . .

I understand you have difficulty bringing information together.

= . . . .

But there's more to it than that, isn't there?

= . . . .

Naturally, it's possible to transform files from your present system.

= . . . .

In that case you could take advantage of ...

= . . . .

You just input the appropriate data.

= . . . .

Information is accessible by any number of PCs simultaneously – a substantial plus.

= . . . .

PAY OFF

Phase One

1.1 Role-play Convince a colleague of the advantages of a word processor over a typewriter or some similar comparison. Use the 'sales patter' you studied in FOLLOW UP **3.1**. Your colleague will be sceptical like Newman.

Before you begin, list the advantages and facilities you wish to emphasize.

Phase Two

2.1 Brainstorm When acquiring computer hardware or software, what factors should a company consider?

2.2 Group your factors under headings such as:

FINANCIAL, OPERATIONAL, ADMINISTRATIVE, etc.

2.3 Give each factor a weighting between 0 and 5.

◆ Which are the five most important factors?

◆ Which umbrella heading scores highest?

2.4 Discussion Present your conclusions to your colleagues. Be prepared to justify your weightings.

AUDIT

Checklist

in a nutshell (metaphor) = summarized very briefly
  e.g. *Our problem, in a nutshell, is that we can't integrate data.*

off the top of my head = from memory
  e.g. *Off the top of my head, I should say we have about eight thousand active accounts.*

that's not the end of it (colloquial) = that is not the only problem/cost/consideration, etc.

What's the damage? (metaphor and colloquial) = What is the cost?

pretty much the same (colloquial) = more or less/roughly/almost identical.
  e.g. *These computers are pretty much the same. They married at pretty much the same age.*

no wonder = It's not surprising that …
  e.g. *No wonder you are having difficulties. No wonder he's tired.*

like now (colloquial nonstandard) = very urgently. 'Like' is used as an intensifier and implies the need for immediate compliance with an order.
  e.g. *Gray will take his business elsewhere if I can't get the order out, like now!*
  Cf. *You had better move your car from in front of my garage, like fast!*

it's got to be (colloquial) = it should be, it has to be
  e.g. *It's got to be just what we need. It's got to be up to you.*

to (verb) no end (colloquial intensifier) = to (verb) considerably
  e.g. *It speeded up their paperwork no end.* = It speeded up their paperwork considerably.
  She has improved her game no end. = She has greatly improved her game.

hellishly (adv) (colloquial) = very

to throw something into someone's lap (metaphor) = to pass a problem on to someone else

Phrase bank

BUSINESS:	
a computer listing	out of stock
a stores record	a major advantage
a local area network	**SOCIAL:**
a central file server	
a PC	its up to you/her/them, etc.
a basic line	as a matter of fact
an active account	**GENERAL:**
paperwork	
data	compatible (adj)
credit status	slight (adj)
to subcontract	in the long run
to access	
	to run into something/someone
to be up to the job	to trace something/someone
to speed things up	to integrate something/someone
	to link up with someone/something

Main focus

Demonstrating a product's advantages

All you need to do is hold the data centrally.

You simply put in the relevant information.

You can put in anything you like.

It will cost you less in the long run.

Later on you may be able to upgrade further.

Editions Comenius

GROUNDWORK

Phase One

1.1 You are going to see a short excerpt of a video presentation. While viewing consider:

- ♦ What the presenter is trying to sell.
- ♦ Whom he is addressing.
- ♦ Any special features of his offer.
- ♦ The name of his company.
- ♦ What it might be like to work with the presenter.

▶ Watch the first part of scene 1 up to the end of the presentation on the video monitor **only**. Then compare your answers with your colleagues.

1.2 Discussion Prepare briefly to say something about **either** partworks **or** continuity promotions. Then report back to your colleagues.

> **PARTWORKS**
>
> - ♦ What are 'partworks'?
> - ♦ Give some examples marketed in your country.
> - ♦ How are these products usually promoted and distributed?
> - ♦ What pattern of sales would you expect throughout such a promotion?

> **CONTINUITY PROMOTIONS**
>
> - ♦ What is a 'continuity promotion'?
> - ♦ What kinds of products are suitable for promoting in this way?
> - ♦ Give some examples of continuity promotions that have been successful in your country.
> - ♦ What is the advantage of such a promotion to the retailer?

Phase Two

2.1 Comenius wishes to sell high quality partworks in supermarkets through a continuity promotion. How do you think supermarkets will react to this idea? What questions will they ask?

2.2 ▶ Watch, **without sound**, the reactions of the two viewers up to the end of scene 1.

What do you think they are saying to each other?

What is their relationship?

2.3 ▶ Watch the scene again *with sound* and check your impressions. Complete the statements for each character.

I think it'll work, anyway . . . .   *Quality books in supermarkets?* . . . .

. . . .

We know about . . . .   *For Europe maybe,* . . . .

. . . .

We can use . . . .   *What do we know about* . . . . ?

. . . .

That's precisely what . . . .   *I bet it* . . . .

. . . .   *All they're interested* . . . .

                                                            . . . .

Phase Three

3.1 ▶ Watch scene 2 up to the moment when the introductions are interrupted by a phone call. Summarize verbally the information you have gathered so far.

PEOPLE

• names   • jobs   • nationalities   • attitudes

BUSINESS SITUATION

♦ What is the purpose of this meeting?   ♦ What problems do you foresee?

NUTS & BOLTS

Phase One

1.1 *So try to be positive, Cecilia – please?*

Summarize what you know so far about the Comenius project. Cecilia is negative about all these points. What are her objections?

PRODUCT LINES	MARKET TARGETED	PRICING POLICY	DISTRIBUTION OUTLETS
CECILIA ANDREWS' OBJECTIONS			

30

1.2 Here is Victor Bender's conversation with Cecilia Andrews about his project. Read through the dialogue. [▶] Then watch this sequence of the video *without sound*. From what you already know about Cecilia's objections try to complete her part of the dialogue.

Bender: *Your boss has spoken very highly of you. How long have you been working here?*

Andrews: . . . .

. . . .

Bender: *What doubts?*

Andrews: . . . .

. . . .

Bender: *Good of you to tell me. What do you see as a problem?*

Andrews: . . . .

. . . .

Bender: *That's why we came to you to find out. You must realize that we have no experience in North America.*

Andrews: . . . .

. . . .

Bender: *Splendid – so let's find out. Where do you want to begin?*

Andrews: . . . .

. . . .

Bender: *I'm not so sure you are right …*

Andrews: . . . .

. . . .

Bender: *So you think that the project may be over-ambitious for this market?*

Andrews: . . . .

. . . .

Bender: *Well, we had the same objections in Europe and yet we've managed to overcome them. In fact, we have done particularly well in Austria.*

1.3 Now act out your dialogue with a colleague.

1.4 [▶] Watch this dialogue *with sound*. What differences were there between the language you used to express Cecilia's objections and the language used in the video? Note any new expressions.

Phase Two

2.1 Vocabulary building [▶] Watch scenes 1 and 2 again up to this point. Try to find words or expressions with the same or similar meaning as the words and expressions in column 1. Write them in column 2.

1 DEFINITION	2 WORD OR PHRASE USED IN VIDEO
basically	
to be frank	
succeeded	
receptive	
a lot	

risk	
brisk business	
postal sales	
group	
steady	
view	
summary	

Phase Three

3.1 The thirteen frames below summarize Bender's overview of Comenius's operation in Europe.
▶ Watch scene 2 from **Cecilia**: *... why don't you give me an overview of your operation there?* Note below each frame the words Bender uses to introduce each idea.

Well, we began ... .

  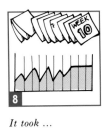 

. . . . *It took ...* . . . .

. . . .

FOLLOW UP

Phase One

1.1 ▶ Watch the sequence again and see how Andrews responds while Bender is giving the overview. It is very important in English to show that you are listening. What expressions does Andrews use to show this?

1.2 Now practise giving an overview of Comenius's European operation using the picture prompts and the notes you made in NUTS & BOLTS **3.1**.

Phase Two

▶ Watch the complete video sequence, before starting this phase.

2.1 After his meeting with Andrews and Callison, Bender wrote to Bower Marketing

Consultants to summarize his company's requirements and the terms of reference. Complete his letter, checking if necessary with the transcript.

Editions Comenius
23 Avenue du Théâtre
1000 Lausanne, Suisse
Téléphone (021) 27 58 48
Télécopie (021) 27 38 46

23 April 1990
Mr Robert Callison
Bower Marketing Consultants (Canada) Ltd.
1109 N. Sheridan Avenue
Montreal, Quebec V26 5P7 Canada

Dear Mr Callison

It was a pleasure to meet you and Ms Andrews last saturday to discuss our North American project.

I am writing to confirm some of the details and terms of reference agreed at that meeting for a feasibility study in the province of Quebec.

I understand you will be writing to me with your exact terms of reference by the end of this week.

Product: . . . .
. . . .
Comenius's general objectives: . . . .
Target markets: * Short-term . . . .
* Medium-term . . . .
Market research strategy: . . . .
Data required: 1 . . . .
2 . . . .
Points to emphasize: 1 . . . .
2 . . . .
3 . . . .
Points to play down: . . . .
Deadlines: 1 . . . .
2 . . . .

I look forward to hearing from you and to receiving your preliminary findings shortly. In the meantime if there is any further information you require, please do not hesitate to contact me.

Yours sincerely

Victor Bender

Victor Bender, Marketing Manager

2.2 When you have completed this letter, practise summarizing the agreement over the phone, using your letter as a prompt.

PAY OFF

Phase One

1.1 Write down in the chart below the last four products you purchased placing them in the appropriate categories according to your reason for buying.

CONSUMER PRODUCTS	CONVENIENCE:
	SHOPPING :
	SPECIALITY:
INDUSTRIAL PRODUCTS	CAPITAL:
	EXPENSE/CONSUMABLE:

1.2 Explain to your colleagues your reasons for classifying your purchases. Would they have classified them in the same way?

1.3 Group with your colleagues and add to the chart the products or services handled by the group's firms.

1.4 Select one of these products for a special promotional campaign.

Phase Two

2.1 Four phases in the life of a product can be identified. Match the phases in column 1, with the SALES/PROFITS descriptions in column 2, and the ADVERTISING strategies in column 3.

1 PHASE	2 SALES/PROFITS	3 ADVERTISING
1 Introduction	Sales rise quickly. Referrals important. Begins to be profitable.	Reminder-oriented: advertising to stress the importance of product.
2 Growth	More intense competition. Consumer products sales' volume declines late in this phase, but industrial sales rise early in phase. Try to get competitor's customers.	Strong promotion to inform customers and create a demand for product.
3 Maturity	Sales and profits fall. Reduced market. Cut prices.	Persuasive and competitive.
4 Decline	Losses rather than profits.	Reminder-oriented: advertising to stress the importance of product

2.2 At which phase in its life cycle is the product you have selected for promotion?

2.3 Which of the following channels of distribution is/are currently used for the product?

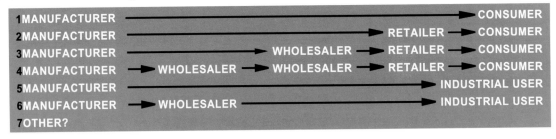

2.4 At which point(s) of the channel(s) is promotion for the product currently targeted?

2.5 Decide where you will target your promotional campaign and how much emphasis you will give to 'pushing' strategy (encouraging middlemen to carry the product) and to 'pulling' strategy (creating or improving consumer demand for the product).

2.6 Now **position** the product. Which market segment do you wish to focus on? Use any of the following categories to help define the market segment:

MARKET LOCATION	AGE
SEX	OCCUPATION
INCOME	LEISURE ACTIVITIES
END USES OF PRODUCTS	OTHER

Phase Three

3.1 Prepare to present your promotional idea for market research under the following headings and then make your presentation to the rest of the class.

PRODUCT	MARKET SEGMENT TARGETED	MARKET INFORMATION REQUIRED
PRODUCT POSITION AND PHASE	PROMOTIONAL IDEA AND STRATEGY	

AUDIT

Checklist

a tough nut to crack (metaphor) = a difficult problem to solve

to do a roaring trade (colloquial) = to enjoy great commercial success
e.g. *Roofers did a roaring trade after the hurricane.*

to test the water (metaphor) = to try out an idea or strategy before adopting it

to give someone a hard time = to create difficulties or problems for a person

to come off = to succeed
e.g. *If her venture comes off, she will be the first woman to fly around the world in a hot air balloon.*

to have one's work cut out = to have already a lot of work to do.
e.g. *She had her work cut out getting the balloon off the ground.*

to put it bluntly (adverbial phrase) = frankly (used before making a very direct comment about something)
e.g. *To put it bluntly, I think your plan is rubbish.*

a great deal of / an awful lot of = a large amount/quantity of

legwork (colloquial) = travelling about and making visits for professional purposes

upbeat = positive in attitude or expression
e.g. *She was very upbeat about her chances of success.*

Phrase bank

BUSINESS/TECHNICAL:	SOCIAL:
a consignment basis a sales pitch a discount a mark-up an advertising campaign a survey an outlet a resource a target date terms of reference a schedule customer loyalty a middle-income group a continuity promotion to play down/up to get in touch with someone to bring someone up to date	I'd like you to meet … Pleased to meet you. Would you excuse me for a few minutes? GENERAL: overambitious (adj) a gamble to my way of thinking to speak for itself to supply someone (with something)

Main focus

Expressing reservations

I'm not so sure.

I think I should add that I'm not sure (your strategy is the best one).

I have my doubts.

In my opinion (American consumers) wouldn't (appreciate them).

I bet it won't work.

To my way of thinking (Canada's) a different proposition altogether.

I think you'll find the (market) is (quite different).

Royce-Lytton Foods

GROUNDWORK

Phase One

1.1  Watch scene 1 for the following information.

Where does it take place?

Give the names of two people mentioned.

In the photo, how does the character on the right feel?

What advice does the character on the left give him?

1.2 Discussion If you had to advise an English business person travelling to the Middle East for the first time on business, what would you say about:

* how to behave in a business meeting?
* social manners?

What problems do you foresee?

1.3  Watch Scene 2 up to the point where the meeting is interrupted by a phone call.

Did any of the problems you predicted occur?

Were there any other problems?

Do you have any points to add to the advice you discussed in **1.2** ?

1.4 In this sequence Rutherford twice signals his sense of frustration to Sheikh Sayid. Write down the two phrases he uses. If necessary, watch the video again.

    1 ...

    2 ...

Phase Two

2.1 Try to improve on Rutherford's performance. Rewrite his first dialogue with the Sheikh to show greater intercultural understanding.

Sheikh Sayid: *Mr Rutherford, this is a pleasure. How do you do?*

Rutherford: . . . .

Sheikh Sayid: *Please.*

Rutherford: . . . .

Sheikh Sayid: *I hope you are enjoying your stay in Kuwait.*

Rutherford: ....

Sheikh Sayid: *And where in England do you come from, Mr Rutherford?*

Rutherford: ....

Sheikh Sayid: *Yes, I know Sudbury very well. Magnificent countryside – Constable country?*

Rutherford: ....

Sheikh Sayid: *Coffee?*

Rutherford: ....

2.2 Act out your new dialogue with a colleague.

NUTS & BOLTS

Phase One

1.1 ▶ Watch Scene 2 to complete this entry for Royce-Lytton Foods in World Corporation Profiles. There is one dot per character.

ROYCE-LYTTON FOODS		
Corporate Headquarters	Oulton Industrial Estate . . . . HPS KTL, Great Britain.	
Management	*Managing Director:* Stephen Jones	*Company Secretary:* David Weeks
	Finance Manager: Frederick Murray	*Export Sales Manager:* . . . .
Major Activities	Royce Lytton Foods . . . . . . all kinds of . . . . and are based in . . . . close to the port of Ipswich on the . . . . side of . . . . Established . . . . ago. Royce-Lytton distribute their products to all parts of continental . . . . , where they have been exporting for over	

Phase Two

2.1 Character Match the characteristics with the person: some words may refer to both Rutherford and Sayid, others to neither. Be prepared to justify your answers with examples from the video. Add any words to describe the characters.

impatient	stiff
cultured	direct
polite	brusque
task-oriented	cautious
superficial	slow
person-oriented	insensitive
businesslike	rude
sociable	frustrated
cold	time-wasting
disrespectful	familiar
disorganized	impersonal
formal	flattering

2.2 Word study Put the adjectives in **2.1** on page 37 in the appropriate columns below. Indicate any pairs which are opposites (≠) or similar (≡) in meaning.

NEGATIVE	NEUTRAL	POSITIVE

Phase Three

3.1 Knowing our business contact's language, and the customs and manners of their country all help us to communicate better. It is also useful to know something of the cultural background of their country. What examples of this kind of intercultural understanding can you quote from scene 2?

3.2 Imagine you are advising Rutherford. In your opinion what would be the best way to react to the following situations. Give the exact words you would use.

Sayid tells you that his company has many business interests all over the gulf, including property, hotels, etc.

You: . . . .

. . . .

Sayid tells you his company owns the hotel you are staying in and has changed your room to a more comfortable one.

You: . . . .

. . . .

Sayid tells you he is interested in a joint venture to set up poultry production in the Middle East. You wanted to start off initially by exporting your products to the region.

You: . . . .

. . . .

3.3 ▶ Watch scenes 2 and 4. Compare your advice with Rutherford's actual reactions.

FOLLOW UP

Phase One

1.1 Vocabulary building As he has to stay longer than expected in Kuwait, Rutherford faxes home to explain the delay. Complete the fax using words and expressions from the box below.

going	rush	pace	production
tied up	clinch	get	hatchery
force	jump the gun	getting on	cautious
committment	small	stood	frustrated

FACSIMILE TRANSMISSION   DATE: **20 November 1989**
FROM: **John Rutherford, Hotel Semiramis, Executive Suite 3**   FAX No.: **251860**
TO: **Stephen Jones, Royce-Lytton Foods, Hadleigh, UK**   FAX No.: **44 473 324780**
RE: **Middle East Exports – KTC**

MESSAGE

You are probably wondering how I'm . . . . I'm sorry not to have contacted you, but things move at a different . . . . here, and although I was hoping to get a deal . . . . quickly, it has taken much longer than I expected.

For the first few days I felt totally . . . . I didn't know what was . . . . on, nor where I . . . . I couldn't seem to get a . . . . from anyone, and, in fact it took me virtually a whole day just to . . . . to see Sheikh Sayid.

Having been advised not to . . . . the pace, I have been quite . . . . with KTC. So you can imagine my surprise when Sayid told me he wanted to set up a . . . . and . . . . facilities with us here. Not wanting to . . . ., I am hoping to . . . . a more modest deal with KTC initially, and have told Sayid that Royce-Lytton would not want to . . . . into anything. After so much . . . . talk and beating about the bush, I am surprised to have achieved anything at all, but am hopeful I shall be able to report to you with details of an initial order by tomorrow morning.

Please could you let me have by return DCP Kuwait and FOB Stansted rates (high tonnage).

Regards – JR

Phase Two

2.1 Role-play With a colleague role-play a telephone conversation in which, as Commercial Attaché in Kuwait, you give background information on KTC to Rutherford prior to his visit there. Add any advice you think will be useful about doing business in the Middle East. Prepare by completing the notes below.

COMMERCIAL ATTACHÉ

Make notes on KTC. Refer to the video
or transcript if necessary.

Main trading interests:	Special requirements:

Activities in food trade:	Personal information about Sheikh Sayid:

Prospects for frozen poultry in Middle East	Advice on doing business in Middle East: (Use: There's no need to … /I wouldn't …)

RUTHERFORD

Ask About:

1. Background information on KTC

2. KTC's food interests

3. General prospects for frozen poultry in region

4. Sheikh Sayid - does the Attaché know him personally?

5. Any special technical or business advice?

PAY OFF

*'Follow the unfailing international success principles: persisting, building
relationships/ learning the culture, choosing partners
carefully … . Spend time. Listen. Visit, only half purposefully
at first. Make friends. Keep cool. Be patient.'*
Source: **Thriving on Chaos by Tom Peters**

Phase One

1.1 Using information in the video and your own personal experience and knowledge, make
brief notes comparing Arab and British cultures under any of the following headings.
Discuss these as a group to build up a cultural sketch of the Arabs and the British.

1 VERBAL AND NON VERBAL LANGUAGE	ARAB CULTURE	BRITISH CULTURE
1 appropriate dress for business		
2 behaviour as a guest and as a host		
3 greetings/use of titles/importance of status		
4 acceptability of physical contact/eye contact.		
5 importance of praise/flattery		
6 meaning of 'yes' and 'no'		
7 acceptability of silence		
8 Any taboos?		
2 ATTITUDE TO TIME AND SPACE		
1 emphasis on past, present or future		
2 task or person-oriented in business		
3 attitude to punctuality, and deadlines		
4 importance of fast decision making		
5 importance of personal privacy		
6 use of office space according to status		
7 acceptable physical distance between people discussing business		
3 EXCHANGING INFORMATION/TAKING DECISIONS		
1 Can business be mixed with social activities?		
2 Who takes the decisions in a firm?		
3 How should bosses behave towards their subordinates?		
4 Is confrontation acceptable?		
5 Is it important to be able to speak well to influence a decision?		
6 When bargaining, how far is the starting price from the acceptable price?		
7 When requesting a quotation, does one ask for higher or lower quantities than one plans to order?		
8 Can meetings include technicians together with higher ranking managers?		
9 How are meetings conducted: formal/ informal, discussion, exchange of information, argument, confrontation, decisions?		

Phase Two

2.1 International briefing Work with a colleague. You are preparing to brief an overseas business mission hoping to set up a joint venture in *either* your *or* your colleague's country. In discussion with your colleague prepare a short presentation, selecting the most important headings from the table on page 40 as a guide.

AUDIT

Checklist

When in Rome do as the Romans do (saying) = when in a foreign country or different culture, adapt to and observe the local customs

to jump the gun (metaphor from racing, meaning to start before the starter's gun) = to act prematurely, too soon, before the appropriate time

to put one's shoulder to the wheel (metaphor) = to work hard

to force the pace = to hurry something along, to make something move faster than normal
e.g. *During the pay negotiations the trade unions tried to force the pace by going on strike.*

on that score (adv) = in that respect, in connection with that matter
e.g. *The project has plenty of capital so there will be no problem on the financial score.*

to have a sweet tooth = to like sweet foods

to know where one stands = to understand one's position in a situation.
e.g. *We didn't know where we stood in the negotiations because the other side kept changing its offer.*

along the lines of (adv)= resembling, similar to
e.g. *The Mark II is very much along the lines of the Mark I, but more efficient.*

Phrase bank

BUSINESS:	SOCIAL:
a committment a shopping mall a hatchery an increasing demand labelling in principle to slaughter to be based in to tie up/clinch a deal to fulfil conditions	How are you getting on? I hope you are enjoying your stay. It's very good of you to see me. No, I'm fine, thank you.
	GENERAL:
	frustrated (adj) cautious (adj) countryside (n) small talk (n) What is going on? to get to do something to rush into something to spend (time) doing something

Main focus

Advising and reassuring

How are you getting on?

Things happen at a different pace round here.

I expect things are moving.

I wouldn't worry if I were you.

I understand you might find it frustrating.

There's no need to force the pace.

7

Jaudel France

GROUNDWORK

Phase One

1.1 Brainstorm If your company wished to get a share of the North American market, how could it set about achieving this objective?

Phase Two

2.1 ▶ Watch scene 1 up to when the visitor says: *It's always a pleasure to be here.* Complete as much of the table as possible. You should be able to complete all the parts shaded in red.

NAME			
COMPANY			
LOCATION OF HEADQUARTERS			
POSITION IN COMPANY			
MAIN REGIONAL MARKETS			

2.2 Discuss your results with your colleagues and then decide what the professional relationship between the two men is. Tick one or more boxes.

☐ boss and subordinate ☐ counterparts in different companies

☐ directors of the same company ☐ friends ☐ rivals

What are the feelings of the two men? Match feelings and photos.

calm	upbeat
confident	cool
tense	stressed
reassuring	optimistic
worried	apprehensive
relaxed	nervous

. . . .

. . . .

. . . .

Phase Three

3.1 ▶ Watch scene 1 up to **Lang:** *Thank you, Keith. Michèle?* Try to complete the rest of the table in GROUNDWORK **2.1.**

3.2 Was the presentation a success? Why?/Why not?

Write these adjectives next to the photos of the characters they best describe. Some adjectives may apply to more than one character. (Use also the photos in **2.2.**)

patronising

self-satisfied

disappointed

embarrassed

exasperated

aggressive

submissive

. . . .

. . . .

. . . .

3.3 What can you say at this point about the relationship between the three characters? How is it likely to develop?

NUTS & BOLTS

Phase One

1.1 Lang wants to keep the meeting upbeat, but Jeannot is less enthusiastic.
▶ Watch the whole of scene 1. List the 'upbeat' language used in the meeting.

Non-verbal body language can also tell us a lot about people's attitudes. Note any examples you see of upbeat non-verbal signals also. Similarly, note any examples of 'downbeat' body language.

| | UPBEAT (+) | | DOWNBEAT (−) |
	VERBAL	NON-VERBAL	NON-VERBAL
Lang			
Cooper			
Jeannot			

Would the body language you observed have the same meaning in your culture?

Phase Two

2.1 Presenting sales results and forecasts ▶ Watch Cooper's presentation again to complete the graph. Give it a title.

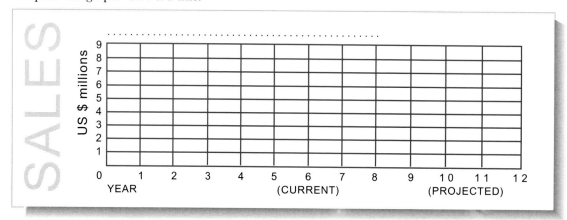

2.2 Finish labelling the piechart.

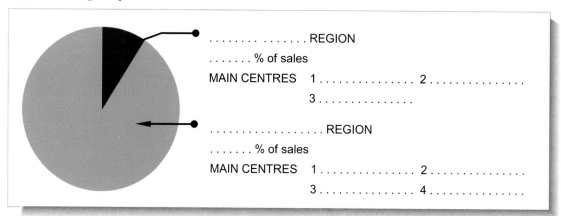

Phase Three

3.1 ▶ Watch Cooper's presentation again to complete these sentences.

- *You'll . . . . that sales have . . . . 13 per cent overall, from . . . .*

  . . . . to . . . . dollars.

- *This area . . . . for . . . . per cent of our sales – the . . . .*

. . . . *per cent comes from our* . . . . *markets.*

- . . . . *we* . . . . *total* . . . . *since year one.*

- . . . . *have* . . . . *every year from $* . . . . *in* . . . .
one to over $. . . . . *at* . . . . *, a* . . . . *increase.*

- *And finally, our* . . . . *of sales* . . . . *the* . . . . *five years.*

- *Five years from now, we* . . . . *sales to reach* . . . .
million . . . . *Thank you.*

3.2 Speculation and prediction Match the sentence halves as they are used in the video:

1 *It might not …*	*a) she'll come round to our way of seeing things.*
2 *I'm sure …*	*b) Michèle Jeannot wants to interpret it.*
3 *You can bet …*	*c) Michèle's going to be too bothered about this.*
4 *I don't think …*	*d) Michèle Jeannot will have read it by now.*
5 *It all depends on how …*	*e) even come up.*

What other combinations are grammatically possible?

FOLLOW UP

Phase One

1.1 Role-play Practise using the language you studied in NUTS & BOLTS *either* to present sales information about your company *or* to present the information about Marks & Spencer below. Use an overhead projector, flipchart or whiteboard to give visual information. Try to be 'upbeat'.

MARKS & SPENCER PLC.
Review of Activities Financial Highlights: Six year summary

Turnover (excl. sales texes) (£m)	5,793.4	5,774.8	5,608.1	5,121.5	4,577.6	4,220.8
Operating profit (£m)	675.8	633.5	627.7	563.7	508.5	434.6
Profit on ordinary activities before tax (£m)	623.5	615.5	604.2	529.0	501.7	423.1
Earnings per share (p)	14.8	14.7	14.5	12.9	12.2	10.4
Dividend per share (p)	7.1	6.7	6.4	5.6	5.1	4.5
Shareholder's funds (£m)	2,670.2	2,427.4	2,174.6	1,918.6	2,158.0	1,578.8
Capital expenditure (£m)	305.4	300.4	280.0	209.7	214.5	247.2

Segmental information: Non-UK turnover	1992 (£m)	1991 (£m)
USA		
Brooks Brothers (including Japan)	180.7	163.2
Kings Super Markets	161.8	153.7
	342.5	316.9
Canada		
Marks & Spencer Division	63.2	73.3
Peoples	54.8	81.4
D'Aillard's	35.6	36.5
	153.6	191.2
Far East	24.9	20.1
Total for the Rest of the World	521.0	528.2

45

Phase Two

2.1 Alone or with a colleague list as many arguments as you can remember to support:

- why Jaudel wishes to market its products throughout the US.

- why Virtue Rubens is against moving into other regional markets.

2.2 Check the transcript to complete your list.

Phase Three

3.1 Complete this letter, using information from the video. One word per space.

Jaudel France

```
Mr Thomas Lang
President & CEO
Virtue Rubens Inc.
36 East 75th Street
New York, N.Y. 10019
USA


22 May, 1989


Dear Mr Lang,
        Michèle Jeannot will already have told you of Jaudel's wish to expand its
marketing . . . . . . . in North America by developing new . . . . . . . markets
there. We see the . . . . . . . and the . . . . . . . as the real . . . . . . .
markets for cosmetics, and, in fact, our own marketing consultants project an average
annual . . . . . . . . in . . . . . . . . of 25 per cent over the next five years if
Jaudel . . . . . . . . . . . . . . . . these fast growing markets.
        Frankly, I doubt whether Jaudel can . . . . . . . . . . . . . . . . . . .
. . . . . . . . . . . . . . . . . its French competitors unless we develop sales outside
the North East. Michèle has told me of your . . . . . . . ., and I know that the
. . . . . . . of this expansion will be . . . . . . . ., but this is clearly
. . . . . . . by the risk of . . . . . . . . . . . . . these markets.
Incidentally, our own consultant's sales projections for the North Eastern markets are
. . . . . . . . . . . . . . . optimistic than yours. It is therefore clearly time
for Jaudel and Virtue Rubens to develop a . . . . . . . together unless Jaudel is
to make . . . . . . . . . . . . . .

        Yours sincerely
```

Pierre Saint-Charles de Vigne

```
        Pierre Saint-Charles de Vigne
        President
```

23 rue de la Ville l'Evêque • 75341 Paris Cedex 08
Téléphone (1) 42.65.21.69 • Télex 621389 • Télécopie (1) 47.63.32.74

3.2 Prepare to role-play a telephone reply to this letter between Tom Lang and de Vigne.

Use the notes you made in **2.1**.

Make some suggestions for the next move.

3.3 **Role-play** Using a telephone extension, or sitting back to back with a colleague role-play this conversation. Recording it if possible.

3.4 **Writing** Write a letter from Lang to de Vigne confirming what was said on the telephone and include any arrangement for the next move.

PAY OFF

Phase One

'… affairs of the heart … hold lessons for the affairs of business …
The challenge of holding together a 'mixed marriage' between
different cultures is formidable.'
Source: **International Management**

1.1 **Discussion** Joint ventures in business are often compared with marriage. In close personal relationships between two people some opinions and attitudes are shared, but there are often differences. Sometimes these differences can strain the relationship or even break it.

♦ List some examples of important issues that can cause differences of opinion in a marriage relationship, e.g. bringing up children, money.

♦ Discuss whether you feel that people's attitudes to these issues depend more on their personality, or on their national culture.

♦ What conclusions can you draw about mixed marriages?

Phase Two

2.1 **Test your cultural attitudes** Much of International business involves negotiating. What are your attitudes to negotiations? How do they differ from those of other nationalities?

Enter a plus (+) in the matrix wherever you think your nationality would agree with the statement. Do the same for another nationality that you know about, or if you are studying in an international group interview one of your colleagues.

NEGOTIATIONS	YOUR NATIONALITY	OTHER NATIONALITY
1 Negotiations are to find the best agreement for both parties.		
2 Negotiations are an opportunity to get the most out of the other side.		
3 Consensus and teamwork are important in negotiations.		
4 We speak directly and do not worry about saving our partner's face.		
5 We trust our partners from the start, but always keep checking that they are respecting the agreement.		
6 We think the best agreement is the one that is most elegantly presented and justified.		
7 We think the best agreement is the one that is most shared and widely accepted.		
8 We do not consider strict implementation of the agreement to be important.		
9 We choose our experts as negotiators.		
10 We choose our negotiators according to their rank in the company.		
11 We are person-oriented.		
12 We are task-oriented.		
13 When negotiating, we start with the overall picture and leave most of the details to look after themselves.		
14 When negotiating, we start with the basic details to arrive at the overall picture.		

2.2 **Discussion** Has your company, or do you know any companies that have ever:

♦ worked on a joint venture with a foreign firm?

♦ worked with a foreign agent or distributor?

♦ been involved in a merger or acquisition with a foreign company?

What were the positive and negative aspects of these partnerships?

How could some of the problems have been avoided?

AUDIT

Checklist

on the rocks (metaphor) = in difficulties, experiencing a crisis
e.g. *Their marriage was on the rocks.*

Butter her up (idiom) = flatter her, tell her what she wants to hear

stick your neck out (metaphor) = make a great effort and take risks to do something for someone

to shrug something off = to treat a problem very lightly, as if it is not a problem at all, to 'shrug is to raise both shoulders in a gesture which in some cultures means: 'It's not important'.

It's all yours (informal) = It is now your turn to speak or perform.
e.g. *I've done as much as I can with this case, now it's all yours.*

We're talking minuses here (colloquial) = We should expect to see losses in this case. We're talking (+ plural noun) is an expression used to emphasize a point.
e.g. *You don't realize what a great opportunity this is. We could be talking millions of dollars, here!*

to agree to disagree = to recognize that we disagree, and to stop further discussion about an issue

First I've heard of it (colloquial) = I did not know this.

We made it into the trade papers (colloquial) = We succeeded in getting an article about ourselves in the specialized journals of our industry.

everything's under control (colloquial) = everything is functioning correctly and according to plan

Phrase bank

BUSINESS:	SOCIAL:
a prediction	How was your flight?
an expansion	Lovely to see you.
a regional market	It's always a pleasure to be here.
a product line	Won't you sit down?
a break down	a good starting point
sales revenue	
astronomical (adj)	**GENERAL:**
negligible (adj)	
fourfold (adj)	upbeat (adj)
speculative (adj)	overall (adj or adv)
nationwide (adj)	
profitwise (adv)	to minimize something
	to have someone come up with
to launch	something
	to dream of someone/something
to bet	to undertake something
to account for	to be bothered about something
to broaden one's base	
to get down to business	

Main focus

Future conditions

If you move into the Sunbelt, the costs will be astronomical.

We cannot survive unless we develop our sales outside the North East.

To open up new markets in the Sunbelt and the West, would lead to a long period of unprofitability.

If you decided to do this, we certainly couldn't dream of becoming involved with anything as big.

Growth could be substantially increased if we sell in the West.

Unless we expand our markets, sales may be down by as much as half a million.

8

Microtron Italy

GROUNDWORK

Phase One

1.1 Brainstorm If your company faced a sudden increase in demand for its product and could not satisfy this demand with its present production facilities, what alternatives could it consider?

Report back to your colleagues with your alternatives.

1.2 Now consider with your colleagues how falling prices for your product would affect your decision.

Phase Two

2.1 [▶] Watch Scene 1 *without the sound*. Each of the texts below is spoken in Scene 1 by one of the characters in the photos. Try and write under each photo the numbers of the texts which you think that character speaks.

Name: .... Name: .... Name: ....

1 *I'll tell you my problem. As chief financial officer, I'm not prepared to commit that kind of money to an overseas division when the risks are so great!*

2 *It's along the beach there at San Clemente, right up on the hills overlooking the ocean.*

3 *Look John, you're not going to start in on that same old argument, are you? Al did a fine job with that report. Try supporting him, or at least keep an open mind!*

4 *Good.*

5 *Now just hold on a minute, John. If you recall, I just wanted you to look the Baroncelli report over. Nothing's been decided yet.*

6 *My idea of paradise!*

7 *Now, take it easy, please.*

8 *Sounds fantastic. Where exactly is it?*

9 *And why? Because they're the most profitable, that's why. I just can't understand your problem.*

10 *Could I have a quick word, Richard?*

11 *Yes, these look fine.*

12 *You aren't really going to back one of these alternatives, are you?*

13 *Risks? What risks, John? The European market is booming. We can hardly keep up with it!*

14 *I was kind of hoping he'd invite us out to San Diego to see this place of his.*

15 *He's bound to have given it some thought, and we can get it straight from the horse's mouth. (on phone) Get me Baroncelli, please.*

16 *Keep an open mind! I ...*

17 *What's on your mind, John?*

18 *It's hardly a failing market, John.*

19 *Well, what about our other divisions? They're simply not getting their fair share of the corporate pie.*

20 *Well, that's encouraging.*

21 *OK John, I see your point. Why don't we get Baroncelli over here and discuss this with him? How does that sound?*

22 *I'm sorry Richard, but more money goes into that subsidiary than any other in the entire group, and you know it, Leslie.*

23 *Fine ...*

2.2 You should now be able to write the first names of each of the characters under their photographs.

2.3 Now put the texts in order to form the dialogue of scene 1.

▶ Watch scene one again **with the sound** to check your dialogue. Try acting it out with your colleagues.

Phase Three

3.1 ▶ Watch scene 1 and scene 2 up to **Brewer:** ... *obviously want to grow with that market.* Which of the following are true statements or representations about the situation at Microtron? Circle T (true) or F (false) as appropriate.

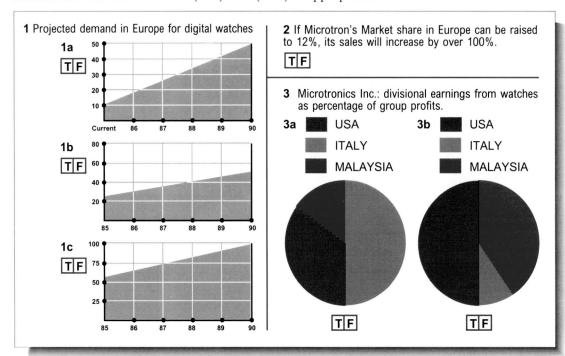

1 Projected demand in Europe for digital watches

1a T F

1b T F

1c T F

2 If Microtron's Market share in Europe can be raised to 12%, its sales will increase by over 100%.

T F

3 Microtronics Inc.: divisional earnings from watches as percentage of group profits.

3a ■ USA ■ ITALY ■ MALAYSIA

3b ■ USA ■ ITALY ■ MALAYSIA

T F   T F

NUTS & BOLTS

Phase One

1.1 ▶ Watch Scene 2 and note down the various options that are proposed. Then complete Brewer's memorandum below. A fourth option is also proposed in the meeting. What is it and who proposes it?

Memorandum

MICROTRONICS INC.
1270 SOUTH OAK ROAD
HOUSTON TEXAS

DATE: October 7, 1985
TO: Alessandro Baroncelli, John Hamilton, Leslie Reeves
FROM: Richard Brewer
RE: Meeting Tuesday 8 October on investment options for Microtron Italy

1. The object of the meeting will be come up with . . . . for
the . . . . to consider regarding investment in the Italian division in order to keep pace with projected
growth in the European . . . . market over the next . . . . years.
2. We have all received a copy of Al Baroncelli's report in which he proposes two s . . . . . . for
overcoming . . . . . . 's limited . . . .
3. In summary these two options are:
   3.1 E . . . .
   3.2 T . . . . another . . . . which . . . . it ,
   g . . . . us . . . .
4. There is clearly a third alternative which we must consider, which is to p . . . . for
. . . .
5. I look forward to your informed evaluation of each of these proposals.

R.B.

1.2 Write the four options in the box below. Then study the arguments for and against each of them.

▶ Watch scene 2 again to place the letter corresponding to each argument in the correct box. Some arguments apply to more than one option.

OPTION:	FOR	AGAINST
1		
2		
3		
4		

A: This project would be profitable in the short term.

B: Stockholders want solutions giving the highest returns.

C: This is a long-term venture for the next decade.

D: Our competitors will gain a technological advantage.

E: loss through European currency movements

F: attractive prospects in Europe

G: The product will become outmoded.

H: There is insufficient space for this.

I: There will be no retained earnings for the shareholders.

J: Not long ago Microtron Italy received capital injection from Microtronics.

K: We have put very little capital into our other divisions.

L: The competition will gain market share at our expense.

M: Economic indicators predict increased demand in Europe.

N: We should continue the commitment we started.

O: The costs will be identical or greater, and we shall have lost market share.

1.3 Now for each argument note down key language actually used to make that point in the video.

FOLLOW UP

Phase One

1.1 The language of meetings Match the phrases in column 1 with those in column 2 to form expressions used in the video for chairing and mediating, interrupting and disagreeing.

1	2
just hold on	business sense
nothing's been	John's ideas
keep	decided yet
take	down please
I see	in here a second
let's settle	your point
there's got to be	a minute
I couldn't	the main issue
it doesn't make	other considerations
there are	an open mind
lets not lose sight of	accept that
let's get back to	the group's overall objectives
could I butt	it easy, please
what exactly do you have	some middle ground
I think we should hear	in mind

Phase Two

2.1 Role-play Select one or more of the options you identified in NUTS & BOLTS **1.1**, or any other options you wish to propose.

Use some of the expressions you studied in NUTS & BOLTS **1.3** and FOLLOW UP **1.1**.

Use the arguments you noted in NUTS & BOLTS **1.2** together with any of your own arguments.

In a meeting with your colleagues argue for your preferred option and against the other proposals.

One person should chair the meeting. This person's role will be to allow all participants to express their opinions, to keep the discussions strictly on the point of the meeting, and to remain impartial.

PAY OFF

Phase One

1.1 Capital investment fund allocation meeting For the purposes of this activity assume that your and your colleagues' companies are all subsidiaries of Business Assignments International Inc. (BAI). You will be meeting with your colleagues in order to put forward investment proposals that will benefit your subsidiary and BAI. The sum available for investment projects this year is very limited, so it is likely that only one proposal will be supported. Prepare a brief project proposal for investment in your own company (or department) and then argue for it at the meeting.

Complete the proposal form below and circulate it to your colleagues and to the chairperson before the meeting.

Business Assignments International Inc. INVESTMENT PROJECT PROPOSAL SUMMARY

Name of subsidiary:	Product or service:				Capital requirement:
SUMMARY OF PROJECT	**ROI (5 years)**				**Total present value:**
	Year	Extra profit	Discount factor 15%	Present value	
	current				**Less cost of capital goods:**
	1				
	2				**Net present value:**
	3				
	4				
	5				Details of projected costs and sales should be available at the meeting.

To be acceptable to BAI's Board, your project must show a good return on investment (ROI) over 5 years. The cost of capital to BAI is 15%, so when calculating the net present value (NPV) of your project you should apply an annual discount factor of 15% over a five year period.

Prepare arguments in favour of your project, and be prepared to answer objections to it. What will be at risk if demand for your product or service is less than you predict?

Prepare the language you will need by looking back over the activities you have completed and by studying the AUDIT section of this unit.

1.2 Chairperson's preparation only As chairperson your job is to propose to the Board the project or projects of greatest benefit to the shareholders of BAI.

BEFORE THE MEETING:

♦ Make sure you receive a completed proposal form from each subsidiary.

♦ Get clarification of any points that are not clear.

♦ Draw up an agenda for the meeting and circulate it to each participant.

♦ Prepare the language you will need by looking back over the activities you have completed, by studying the AUDIT section of this unit, and by watching how Brewer handles the meeting.

DURING THE MEETING:

♦ Introduce the meeting and its purpose.

♦ Follow the agenda and don't allow sidetracking.

♦ Make sure every subsidiary has sufficient opportunity to present its case.

♦ Make sure there is a fair allocation of time for discussion of each proposal.

♦ Bring the meeting to a decision before closing it.

Phase Two

2.1 Meet to present and argue for your project and to discuss your colleagues' projects.

AUDIT

Checklist

a share of the corporate pie (metaphor) = a portion of the benefits (given by the parent company to the subsidiaries)

straight from the horse's mouth (metaphor) = directly from the original source of the information
e.g. *If you want it straight from the horse's mouth, ask Baroncelli, the person who made this proposal.*

by and large (adv) (colloquial) = roughly, generally, approximately
e.g. *Trains run, by and large, every two hours = trains run approximately every two hours.*

bullish (adj.) = optimistic (Cf. bull market = a stock market with an upward trend, and bear market = a stock market with a downward trend)

to get the green light (metaphor) = to get permission to go ahead or to act (from traffic lights)
e.g. *The Channel Tunnel project had to get the green light from both the French and British governments before the contracts could be signed.*

You've got to be crazy (colloquial) = You must be mad. (rather strong)

to drag one's feet (metaphor) = to move at a slow pace, to be reluctant to do something

investmentwise (adv) (colloquial) = in the way of or concerning investment. (The suffix **wise** is used in clockwise, likewise, crosswise and can sometimes be used with other nouns to generate adverbs.)

to hit a snag (colloquial) (metaphor) = to encounter a problem

to butt in (metaphor) = to interrupt (a conversation)

Phrase bank

BUSINESS:		GENERAL:
an overseas division	to trade off something for something	partial (adj)
a failing market	to keep an open mind	biased (adj)
currency fluctuation	financially speaking	obsolete (adj)
a unit	X has got a point	
a projected demand	to clear up a point for someone	to lose sight of something
a concept	to get away from the subject	to go for something
	to get back to the main issue	to be bound to have done something
a plant		to come up with something
an outlay	SOCIAL:	to renovate something
hardware		to jeopardise something
middle ground	What's on your mind?	to postpone something
viability	Could I have a quick word?	
booming (adj)	Hold on a minute.	
	Take it easy!	
to double something	Settle down.	

Main focus

Participating in and chairing meetings

Now just hold on a minute.

I see your point.

I don't see how we can justify either one of them, financially speaking.

I can't/ couldn't accept that.

John's got a point.

It doesn't make sense.

Suppose … /Supposing … ? What then?

There's got to be some middle ground here.

There are other considerations.

Let's get back to the main issue.

I think we should hear John's ideas.

I believe in its viability.

Transcripts

IPSA INDUSTRIES

Scene 1: John Younger's office in Djakarta

Secretary: Mr Webster, Mr Younger.

John Younger: Paul, good to see you. How was your flight?

Paul Webster: Fine. I thought I'd just drop in to thank you for the bumf you sent and for sorting out the hotel.

Younger: Just a banker doing his job. Remember, I'm after your account!

Webster: Well, thanks anyway.

Younger: My pleasure. Well now, I've fixed up something for this evening. Someone you ought to meet. Jim Banes.

Webster: Banes? Doesn't sound terribly Indonesian.

Younger: He's an Australian. One of the key people in your line. He's one half of a joint venture. You've got to have a partner out here, otherwise you can't operate at all.

Webster: So I gather – much the same in a lot of places.

Younger: Quite. Well, his partner is Adnan Basiroen. Now, they call themselves the Sujarwo Trading Company. They deal with anything to do with wood: band saws, de-barking machines, resins for the plywood trade.

Webster: Not hand-held chain-saws though?

Younger: Not as far as I know. By the way, if you think you can do a deal with Banes, you'd better move pretty fast.

Webster: Oh?

Younger: Bleckenbauer – they're in your line of country aren't they?

Webster: Forestry equipment, yes ...

Younger: They're out here too. You'd better catch Banes before he signs with them.

Webster: Their stuff's too sophisticated. Our product's much better for this market.

Younger: Tell that to Banes.

Scene 2: A Djakarta restaurant

Banes: ... Anyway this fellah told me to go and see for myself. Well that was fine, but when I saw the plane he was going to fly us in, I nearly backed off – I mean, it was pre-World War Two! All canvas and wood – and falling apart! Even the pilot was praying as we took off! I mean, I didn't mind seeing the forest but I wasn't too keen on inspecting it at close quarters!

Webster: What are communications like here?

Banes: Pretty rough off the main roads.

Younger: Non-existent on some of the smaller islands. You see Paul, we're talking here of thirteen thousand islands, over three hundred ethnic groups and as many languages. Incredible place Indonesia.

Webster: Sounds like a difficult market.

Banes: Oh, it's OK if you've got someone who knows their way around.

Younger: Yes ... It's absolutely crucial that you find the right distributor ... Well, I'll leave you two gentlemen to talk things over.

Webster: Sure you won't have another drink?

Younger: No, I must dash. I'm late already.

Banes (to waitress, in Indonesian): (Two more beers, please.)
(to Younger): I'll see you sometime next week.

Younger: Yuh.

Webster: Goodbye John, and thanks again.

Younger: Don't mention it. See you.

Banes (to Younger): See you later.
(to Webster): Cheers ... Right, fire away.

Webster: OK ... How do you deal with a market this complex?

Banes: You've got to have good Indonesians working with you, and I don't just mean in the office, I mean out in the field, pushing the deals through. My partner Adnan's terrific.

Webster: And what's the state of the timber business here? What are the prospects?

Banes: Well, back in the seventies everyone was exporting logs. Then the government urged timber firms to move into the finished wood products – plywood. Seemed like a good idea – more added value – but then world prices slumped. Added to that, there was the big forest fire of '83 which hit our timber reserves. Well that, combined with soaring energy prices, made a lot of firms feel a little, er-exposed.

Webster: It doesn't exactly sound rosy for forestry equipment sales, does it?

Banes: There's been a big shake-out in the whole timber business in the past few years.

Webster: Cutting away the dead wood? Any noticeable improvement?

Banes: Look Paul, wood's such a big earner here. it's bound to keep going in one form or another.

Webster: So, there is a future here – and you've got the organization to deal with our product. What about contacts? Say, in the government? I suppose it's worthwhile having good contacts there?

Banes: Absolutely essential – without top-level contacts in the Ministry of Forestry you'd get nowhere.

Webster: I would guess that you rely a lot on government contracts?

Banes: Yuh, but we deal with a hell of a lot of private mills as well. There's a sizeable market there, Paul – though not quite for your type of product.

Webster: Sure. Tell me, what *are* the chances for our stuff here?

Banes: We've been selling the heavy gear – power saws and the like, so we're well established in the business. But we've never dealt in hand-held chain saws before.

Webster: D'you see any problems?

Banes: You've got to have good maintenance and service back-up. We've always offered that on guarantee.

Webster: Do you do the servicing yourselves?

Banes: Oh yes, you can't rely on contractors, they haven't got to make the next sale. Anyway, the main thing is, our customers won't sign an order without a guarantee for parts and service. That's always been one of our key selling points.

Webster: Are we talking about imported products here, or local manufacturers?

Banes: Imports make up the largest proportion; there's no manufacturing base of any size here – yet. It's coming up fast though – the government's doing all it can to encourage it – but in the main there's no choice but to buy foreign products.

Webster: And what about IPSA? Are we in with a chance?

Banes: Ah well, if you can be competitive with the Japanese on price, yeah, you're in with a chance.

Scene 3: Jim Banes's office, Djakarta

Webster: ... Your knowledge of the market here, your contacts – that's so valuable to us. But if you were ever to represent one of our direct competitors, then we'd have problems.

Banes: Look Paul, we represent American, Australian, Filipino and Japanese firms. All on a non-exclusive basis. And quite frankly, that's how we prefer it.

Webster: What about European firms?

Banes: Well, it's only fair to warn you that, er, we're talking to one firm right now.

Webster: Yes, Bleckenbauer, I know.

Banes: Right – and they're not asking for any exclusivity deal like you are.

Webster: Will you be representing them?

Banes: Nothing's been decided yet. There are – how shall we say? – one or two knotty problems.

Webster: I can well understand that. You've seen IPSA's products. You've got to agree that they suit the local conditions better than anything Bleckenbauer can offer.

Banes: Maybe, but there are other things to consider.

Webster: Our product requires less maintenance and servicing – distributors and operators need very little technical training. Now, could you say that about Bleckenbauer?

Banes: Well no, but ...

Webster: Look Jim, our fastest growing and most profitable markets are in the tropics. We've been selling into Africa for years and we've got equipment working in Malaysia and Thailand – similar conditions to here. Bleckenbauer have no such track record.

Banes: But you're asking for us to be exclusive distributor.

Webster: Right, and we'd like you to carry a full inventory of products and parts.

Banes: And that means a considerable investment on our part.

Webster: Which, if I'm not mistaken, Sujarwo are just about ready for.

Banes: Well, that's as maybe. But we haven't got money to throw away. We need the right kind of investment. I'll need more facts and figures, Paul.

Webster: I can get you all the information you need by tomorrow ... and John Younger is willing to – shall we say – look favourably on any financing that might be required.

Banes: OK Paul, but I'll be throwing a hell of a list of questions at you.

COUGAR JAPAN

Scene 1: A motorway in England; inside Andrea Connors' car

Bill Gates (on car phone): Mmm, yuh, fine ... OK Hugh, I'm coming out to Korea next week, so I'll stop over in Tokyo and we can talk. Yuh. Cheers then; bye now. (replaces phone) Hugh Nicholson. He's a real pain.

Andrea Connors: What's he up to now?

Gates: He's only trying to tell me that our clothing venture for Japan is premature.

Connors: Did he back that up at all?

Gates: No, he just came out with another scheme of his own – he wants us to take our shoes down market instead!

Connors: Does he, now? Our clothes are doing well enough in Europe, so why not the Far East as well?

Gates: Right, and the Tokyo operation certainly has the potential.

Connors: Well, Nicholson is the man

on the spot. So perhaps he's come up with something more attractive?

Gates: That's not the point. It's a bit late in the day for a complete change of strategy now.

Connors: When do you fly out?

Gates: Next Thursday.

Connors: You'd better call me. Keep me posted on what Hugh has in mind.

Gates: He's always coming out with these wild schemes ...

Connors: Well, sometimes they work out, Bill, you've got to admit that.

Gates: Sure they do, but it doesn't exactly make life easy for the rest of us.

Connors: Developing new markets is never easy, Bill, and if we're going to get faster growth by selling shoes at the lower end of the market, then we should take Hugh's idea seriously.

Gates: I still think we could get a big slice of the Japanese sports clothes market – they expect quality, that's what we offer. Instead of which we've got Hugh talking about going down market.

Connors: It's only a proposal. See what he's got to say about it.

Scene 2: Hugh Nicholson's office, Cougar Japan, Tokyo

Gates: ... So how's your wife, Hugh?

Hugh Nicholson: She's fine. The kids are just beginning to get settled in over here – it takes a while.

Gates: Sure. How long have you been here now?

Nicholson: Nearly two years.

Gates: Mmm. You like it here, don't you?

Nicholson: Yuh. It's a bit difficult to begin with, but it grows on you. I know my way round pretty well now.

Gates: Mmm.

(Yoshio Saito enters)

Nicholson: Ah, I don't believe you two have met before. This is Yoshio Saito, our sales analyst.

Gates: How do you do?

Yoshio Saito: How do you do?

Nicholson: As I told you before, I've asked Saito-san to give a short presentation of our alternative marketing plan.

Gates: Fine.

Saito: Perhaps I should stress first of all that this game plan isn't meant to exclude the possibility of breaking into the sports clothes market at a later date. Our deviation from established group strategy doesn't concern the goal itself, but simply how and when we get to it. So we really have to look at two questions:

Why go down-market now? Why not diversify now? The answer to the first question really concerns developments in the Japanese consumer market; the second question is about problems of distribution. I'd like to give you an overview of both before going into a little more detail on each.

So, first off, why go down-market now? Well, the Japanese market is, in many respects, surprisingly similar to our European markets where the group strategy has been tried and tested. We all know it's bigger – bigger than Britain and Germany put together, in fact. There are 120 million consumers out there, and we could be getting to all of them, as a full-line distributor.

The second point here is that those lower and middle segments of the market offer extraordinary opportunities right now. The Japanese look set to have more leisure time and probably more money to spend in the near future.

Gates: This is all very interesting but I don't see how it supports your strategy. If people have more to spend, they could just as easily go out and buy the high-price top-end-of-the-market products we already offer, which would include our top-quality sports clothes.

Saito: Point taken. But right here and now there's no disguising where the really healthy growth markets are in Japan – in those middle and lower segments. Perhaps I could come back to that in a moment.

So, why not diversify now? The first point here is really that Japanese distributors – and remember the distribution system here is far more complex than in any of our other markets – simply expect a long-term commitment from a supplier. They're especially sensitive to sudden changes or, worse, unavailability of products that they are planning to build on. No matter how reliable we are, we will be viewed with caution until we have established the Cougar name in the market.

Gates: Look, I hate to interrupt again, but surely Cougar Japan can persuade distributors that all our products will be fully supported. I know it isn't easy to get distributors to accept product diversification: there's always resistance, but you've got to overcome it with hard work, marketing, promotion – it's what you guys are paid for, yuh? It's worked in our other markets.

Saito: I would agree with your arguments absolutely, but I would add that the best promotional argument of all is the proven ability to understand Japanese business practices and to meet their expectations. The Japanese distributor is looking for signs that the supplier will commit himself long-term to the market and that his aim is the development of market share – the source of long-term profits. And the best place to generate profit right now is where we at Cougar Japan would like to go-down market into the medium and lower price ranges of sports shoes.

Scene 4: Hugh Nicholson's office.

Nicholson: I haven't brought you round to my proposal, have I?

Gates: I'm afraid not, Hugh. I'm convinced our future's with sports clothes and Japan's crucial to that strategy. We're looking at a golden opportunity to increase our revenue here.

Nicholson: Sure Bill, we need to build things up, but I think we should build on the success we have – shoes.

Gates: Well, to be frank I don't think your proposal sounds feasible.

Nicholson: Oh, come on. You've seen the facts and believe me, we've done our homework. Japan's a different ball-game altogether. What works in Europe won't necessarily work here.

Gates: Why don't you let me be the judge of that? Group marketing strategy is my responsibility.

Nicholson: But I don't think you realise what a complex market Japan is. Now, in shoes we have a very good chance of becoming a full-line distributor – we'd get a reasonable share of a growing market. All we need is a little time and some money.

Gates: Two commodities of which I have very little to offer.

Nicholson: Look Bill, we'll be risking our market image by introducing new products. It'll confuse the customer.

Gates: Hang on, Hugh, what're you talking about? Confusion. You'll certainly confuse people if you suddenly go down-market in shoes. And another thing, your competitors will hit back hard – but they won't follow you into sports clothes.

Nicholson: No they won't, they'll go straight for our share of the shoe market while we go down a blind alley with clothing. Bill, believe me, I know the market here, and the key to success is simply market share. And Cougar doesn't stand a chance unless it adds more shoes at the low end of the range.

Gates: I'm not going to pull any punches, Hugh. Andrea will never accept the change of strategy you're proposing.

Nicholson: As far as Japan's concerned, I call going into sportswear a change of strategy, and a dangerous one at that.

Gates: I don't think there's any point in pursuing this. We're established in Japan, we've got the kind of market we want in sports shoes … Now's the time to diversify.

Nicholson: I know I'm sticking my neck out but I tell you things are different here. Your plan doesn't stand a chance.

Gates: And you think handling a full range of shoes would work better?

Nicholson: Absolutely.

Gates: No Cougar branch handles that kind of shoe range. We're up market, we're going to stay up market.

Nicholson: Bill, I'm sorry, I simply can't agree.

CHOCOLATS MEMLINCK

Scene 1: Eileen Haberland's office, Boston

Paul Van Houton: My mother told me never to accept sweets from strangers.

Eileen Haberland: Come on, Paul. This is serious. Start with that one.

Van Houton: Mmm. That was OK.

Haberland: How about this one?

Van Houton: The cream's a little on the sour side. Beyond its shelf life I'd say.

Haberland: Uh-huh.

Van Houton: This one has an aftertaste. Perfectly good to start with, but a kind of woody aftertaste.

Haberland: Last one …

Van Houton: Mmm. That's fine, too sweet for my taste. It's not one of ours, is it?

Haberland: Pretty good, Paul. The first is part of a consignment that arrived last night. So it should have been OK. The second still has five days' shelf life left – or should have. It's part of a batch we shipped to our Georgetown store to test customer reaction down there. Luckily it was only the one carton that went bad.

Van Houton: Well, we were lucky then. How could it have happened?

Haberland: My guess is it spent half an hour in the sun somewhere along the line.

Van Houton: That's worrying though.

Haberland: Sure is, so the third is the remedy we tried – minute quantities of natural preservative – just enough to bump the shelf life up to thirty-one days. And you noticed an aftertaste.

Van Houton: I'm afraid I did …

Haberland: You were also correct on the last one. It isn't one of ours. It's from The Charleston Collection. It's an American product, very up-market. And as you noticed, sweeter that our own Old Masters.

Van Houton: What is it you're trying to say to me, Eileen?

Haberland: Two things – shelf life is one. This is the first time we've shipped outside of New England. I'd hardly call it an unqualified success. What happens if we send shipments out West? In my opinion we have to find an acceptable way to make the product last longer.

Van Houton: I see what you're getting at Eileen, but it's the question of expense. It could send our costs too high. And we're already a little price sensitive.

Haberland: OK, Paul. Point two: the American market. Now I like your chocolates, and clearly sales indicate that a lot of other people do too. The thing is, Americans generally prefer their chocolates smaller and sweeter. I was wondering if, on some of the range, we couldn't make a few concessions to their taste?

Van Houton: No Eileen. I can't accept that. Tradition is our selling point. Traditional Belgian chocolates – fresh. If we tried to compete with American practice – additives, preservatives, high sugar content – we'd be lost. Can't you see that?

Haberland: Yeah, I know, Paul. I thought that's what you'd say. So let's concentrate on the shelf life issue. If we don't crack that, we're not going to get off the ground in the US.

Van Houton: Well, I'd like to take a look at your delivery operation. I'd like to know more about your distribution set-up. Maybe there are a few bugs that could be taken out of that?

Haberland: Maybe – but what it boils down to is costs.

Van Houton: What are we talking about? Road? Rail?

Haberland: We have a contract with a truck line – they deliver to all our stores. We could try and do a deal for special delivery, but it pushes up unit costs, as you well know, Paul.

Van Houton: I understand, Eileen, of course I do, but there must be a way round this problem.

Haberland: If there is, then we'll find it.

Van Houton: Good. Tell me, do you have any data on the average customer purchase so far?

Haberland: Yuh. Each store … is averaging … yup, here it is – is averaging a little over sixty purchases a week. That works out to around twenty-two ounces per customer.

Van Houton: That sounds good.

Haberland: That's based on store traffic of between three and a half to four thousand customers per week. There's still plenty of room for growth.

Van Houton: And have you reached a decision on regular quantities yet?

Haberland: We know what we'd like to do, but we're going to have to talk about price first.

Van Houton: I don't have any leeway on price, Eileen. Wessner's get the highest markup of all our customers.

Haberland: I'm not surprised. A perishable import like fresh chocolate carries high transport and even higher insurance costs. It's an expensive item for us to carry.

Van Houton: I grant you that but I'd hate to see our prospects in the US ruined by overpricing.

Haberland: I hear you Paul, I hear you. But we feel we're reading the market pretty well and it isn't easy since there are plenty of very fine home-grown products in there too.

Van Houton: I know that. The thing is Eileen, I've got bad news on that front.

Haberland: Uh-oh …

Van Houton: There's a price rise in the pipe-line.

Haberland: Paul, you just said …

Van Houton: I'm sorry. But we've been negotiating with our employees for the last nine months over their salary increases. We agreed on ten and a half percent. It was that or we'd have a strike on our hands. We just can't absorb all of that ourselves. We have to pass some of it on.

Haberland: Oh, I get it. And you don't want us to pass your increase on to our customers. Is that correct?

Van Houton: Is that possible?

Haberland: Paul, we're being squeezed hard enough as it is. With the dollar slipping like crazy we could find ourselves losing thirty-five percent of our profit!

Van Houton: I realize it isn't easy.

Haberland: Easy? Look, we're prepared to double our order. On condition there is no price increase for a guaranteed period.

Van Houton: No conditions – sorry.

Haberland: Paul, you can't increase the price, otherwise we'll be forced to look elsewhere.

Van Houton: No ultimatums either Eileen, please. Now look, we both want an agreement on this, don't we? (she nods). Then there must be some middle ground.

Haberland: I'm going to need stable prices with adequate early warning on any increase – and a bigger discount, say six percent.

Van Houton: Six?

Haberland: We'd also like to trade on open account.

Van Houton: Now hold on. I'd need a letter of credit. It's company policy.

Haberland: Totally unreasonable if I may say so.

Van Houton: I don't make company policy.

Haberland: All right, Paul, that's fine. It just makes doing business with you that much more complicated, and that much more expensive! Couldn't you make a small concession?

Van Houton: No, it can't be done.

Haberland: OK, no ultimatums, huh? But you've got to see that we can't consider any expansion until we see a decent profit in it.

Van Houton: I'll tell you what I'll do, I'll hold the present price for three months.

Haberland: That's not good enough.

Van Houton: OK, we'll talk around that one – I'll hold the prices if you can guarantee new orders, and I mean a substantial increase.

Haberland: What are we talking about here?

Van Houton: Twenty five to thirty-five per cent – over six months.

Haberland: That'll barely give us time to get a foothold in the market. Could you agree on the price freeze for that period?

Van Houton: I should think so, but you'd have to agree to the top end of the increase in your order – thirty-five per cent . . .

Haberland: I was thinking more in terms of twenty-five.

Van Houton: Thirty – and we have a deal. I'll hold the price for six months, then you can cope with the price rise.

Haberland: Is there any possibility of staggering that?

Van Houton: No, I'm sorry. There isn't.

Haberland: OK. I think we're going to have to accept that. Have another chocolate.

Van Houton: No. I'm going on a diet.

HAL INFORMATION SYSTEMS

Scene 1: A demonstration room, HAL Information Systems

Clare Thomas: Well, if it's everything it says it is, it's got to be just what we need.

Peter Cochran: Mmm. Willoughby's put one in last year. It speeded up their ordering and paperwork no end.

Alan Newman: It's going to be hellishly expensive, and do we really need another computer?

Thomas: It's a question of capacity Alan, our present system just isn't up to the job.

Cochran: It could solve a lot of problems.

Newman: It'd bring a fair share of problems with it in my opinion. Do we have that many problems at Slater's?

Thomas: Well, yes we do. If we don't get a new system, we'll keep on running into the same kind of situation we had last week. Remember?

Scene 2: Clare Thomas's office at Slater Engineering Ltd

Thomas: (on the phone) Hello, Mr Gray? (Yes) Sorry to keep you waiting, we seem to have a slight problem in tracing your order.

Gray: Not again. We may be just another customer to you, but without those parts we can't look after our own customers. We ordered them over a week ago, surely.

Thomas: I know, Mr Gray. I can't understand why this order doesn't appear on our computer listing.

Gray: I thought computers were supposed to speed things up. Look, either you get those parts to us by Friday, or we'll have to look elsewhere. Goodbye.

Thomas: It must be somewhere.

Scene 3: Peter Cochran's office at Slater's

Thomas: We're going to lose this order Peter – I can't find it anywhere.

Cochran: Isn't it on the computer?

Thomas: It should be …

Cochran: What happened? Did it get eaten?

Thomas: The trouble is our data isn't integrated. That order's in there somewhere but I can't find it, and Gray will take his business elsewhere if I can't get the order sent out - like now!

Cochran: I'll look for his original order – on good old-fashioned organic paper.

Cochran: Here we are – forty ninety-eight seals.

Thomas: Brilliant! Thanks.

Cochran: Sorry Clare. I wish I'd been told about this. These seals are out of stock.

Thomas: Then why wasn't it on the computer?

Cochran: Probably is, somewhere – on the stores' records.

Thomas: Oh no! You know, this isn't the first time. Everything's on disk, but we can't link our information up! We're going to have to upgrade, Peter. I'm going to talk to Alan about this.

Scene 4: A demonstration room, HAL Information Systems

Ken Jenkins: Now, this is the menu – the programs available. You say you have problems integrating data?

Thomas: Well, in a nutshell – yes.

Jenkins: So you could use a local area network – that's several PCs with a central file server, like the HAL 900 here, for example.

Thomas: Well, of course, you would say that, wouldn't you?

Jenkins: Well, we are the best. Seriously though, all you need to do is hold all the data centrally with PCs linked up to it. You simply put in the relevant information from all your departments, which is kept on the master file – you can put in anything you like – from unit availability to credit status. And of course you can convert files from your current system.

Cochran: Oh, well that's a relief.

Jenkins: As a matter of fact the HAL 900 uses the same operating system as the PC you've got now. Which means our system will work with yours.

Newman: That's fine, but isn't it just a more expensive system that does pretty much the same as the one we've got?

Jenkins: No, the HAL 900 integrates all the things that you did separately on your PC. Therefore it will cost you less in the long run. And several people can access the data at the same time, which is a major advantage.

Thomas: That would certainly help us.

Jenkins: Also, a cable connects up all the PCs so they can communicate with each other, using the main file server as a central store. Later on you may be able to upgrade further, adding facilities like electronic mail and laser printing.

Newman: Well, that's interesting, but we need to know the sums we're likely to be in for.

Jenkins: Well, the HAL 900 – that's the file server – will cost you about twice as much as a PC.

Newman: But that's not the end of it, is it?

Jenkins: Well, you'd be saving costs because you're already using compatible software, but I'd have to get more information about your business before I could give you a clear costing.

Thomas: Yes, but could you give us some indication? Over fifty thousand or under?

Jenkins: Oh, I think we could well come in under fifty, depending on the system and the number of PCs you need.

Thomas: Well Alan, I think it's got to be up to you to decide this.

Newman: I thought you'd throw it into my lap.

Jenkins: Give me an idea of your product range, Mr Newman, and I'll be able to give you a rough estimate.

Newman: Well, we have four basic lines: lifts, lubrication pumps, vehicle washing machines and control equipment, which we subcontract.

Jenkins: Fine. How many products do Slater's manufacture?

Thomas: Oh, fourteen hundred or more, but that's including the parts – of course we only have nineteen complete products.

Jenkins: How many active accounts do you have?

Newman: Peter?

Cochran: Let's see. Off the top of my head, around eight thousand.

Jenkins: And you've been trying to deal with all that on one PC? No wonder you've been running into problems! Depending on the number of people who want access, I should think you'll need at least four PCs – but balance that against efficiency and costs saved …

Newman: What's the damage going to be?

Jenkins: Er … we're talking … let's see … fifty thousand.

EDITIONS COMENIUS

Scene 1: Bob Callison's office, Montreal

Victor Bender (on TV monitor): … an increase of thirty-five per cent in sales – a result achieved at no risk since all books are supplied on a consignment basis. We, of course, also sold a lot of our books. We feel that the Comenius continuity promotion offers unbeatable returns for a very limited investment of resources. So why not get in touch with me and find out more?

Cecilia Andrews: Quality books in supermarkets? I don't see it, Bob.

Callison: Victor Bender certainly gives a good sales pitch.

Andrews: For Europe maybe, but in Canada I'm not so sure …

Callison: I think it'll work Cecilia – anyway I want this one.

Andrews: OK, you're the boss – but I'm still not sure about it. I mean, what do we know about selling books in Quebec? We'll have to work fast to get a survey done – and do an awful lot of legwork.

Callison: We know about retail food distributors, that's why he came to us. Anyway, we can use a lot of this research again.

Andrews: Well, what about their pricing? I mean Victor Bender may be upbeat about results in Austria but we are talking fifteen-dollar books here, Bob. That may look like an impulse buy in Vienna, but I bet it won't work in Quebec.

Callison: That's precisely what Bender is paying us to find out. So have an open mind about it, OK?

Andrews: Oh, that's fine, but I gather Comenius don't even offer a sales commission. That means I'll have my work cut out just getting the supermarket chains to talk to me! I know these people. All they're interested in is discounts and markups.

Callison: You'll have a chance to ask Bender when he comes in tomorrow. So try to be positive, Cecilia – please?

Scene 2: Bob Callison's office

Callison: These colour photos are outstanding. As a matter of fact, I think the quality of the book is superb, down to the quality of the paper, and the photos, and everything … Oh Victor, this is Cecilia Andrews, our senior researcher.

Bender: Victor Bender.

Andrews: Hello.

Bender: Pleased to meet you.

Callison: Cecilia and I have already talked a bit about your continuity programme.

Andrews: Yes, I was very impressed by your video.

Bender: Thank you.
(The telephone rings.)

Callison: Excuse me. (into the phone) Bob Callison. OK. I'll come through. Would you excuse me for a few minutes? Cecilia, you don't mind starting, OK?

Andrews: No, fine. Have a seat.

Bender: Your boss has spoken very highly of you. How long have you been working here?

Andrews: Oh, about three years. Look, Mr Bender, maybe I shouldn't be saying this, especially with Bob out of the room, but frankly I have my doubts about your continuity programme.

Bender: What doubts?

Andrews: Look, I know we're close to an agreement and everything but, to put it bluntly, you could be wasting your money.

Bender: Good of you to tell me. What do you see as a problem?

Andrews: Well, it seems like you have a perfect product for a European operation, but to my way of thinking Canada's a different proposition altogether.

Bender: That's why we came to you, to find out. You must realise that we have no experience in North America …

Andrews: I know. And I think you'll find the market is quite different from Europe.

Bender: Well – so let's find out. Where do you want to begin?

Andrews: Let's start with the books. Now the standard is pretty high, but in my opinion, North American consumers wouldn't appreciate them.

Bender: I'm not sure you are right …

Andrews: My point is, I'm sure people will be impressed by the books, but will they buy them? They're very expensive, very very up market, and yet we're talking about selling them in supermarkets. Now that could get us into middle, even lower income groups.

Bender: So you think that the project may be over-ambitious for this market?

Andrews: I think there may be difficulty in getting the message across to the target group.

Bender: Well, we had the same objections in Europe and yet we've managed to overcome them. In fact, we have done particularly well in Austria.

Andrews: I know, I got that from your video.

Bender: The thing is, we need to make Comenius more broad based. We want to get into North America. Austria and Quebec province are roughly the same population size. The market, of course, could be quite different. What we want, Miss Andrews, is data to base a final decision on.

Andrews: Well, OK, but you understand I felt it necessary to point out my own doubts.

Bender: Of course.

Andrews: And while we're on the subject, I think I should add that I'm not sure your strategy is the best one. I mean, wouldn't it be better to talk to consumers direct rather than approaching them through supermarket chains as you're asking us to do?

Bender: Mmm – sort of testing the water you mean? It would be expensive if we were to use a big enough sample. No, I think it makes more sense to go to the supermarkets and ask them straight if they're interested – after all, they should know their customers best, and we would be getting their expert opinion.

Andrews: OK. Right. Now, we understand you've been doing a roaring trade in Europe, so why don't you give me an overview of your operation there?

Bender: Of course. Well, we began a little over four years ago in Switzerland. We'd previously been in the mail order business for our books, so we had the product, and we were looking for new markets, (Thank you.) …

Andrews: Mmm.

Bender: We suggested the idea of supermarket sales to the Managing Director of the second largest chain in Switzerland. He seemed amenable and so together we worked out a marketing plan – that is the continuity promotion of the part-work programme in supermarket chains.

Andrews: Uh-huh.

Bender: There was obviously a great deal to be done, so it was first tried in Francophone Switzerland.

Andrews: Which towns?

Bender: Primarily Geneva, Lausanne, Neuchatel. It took ten weeks to stabilize and then the sales of books and the food market began to rise together.

Andrews: Mmm. I see.

Bender: On that first venture we shared the advertising cost, but then as new business came, Comenius took over the advertising campaign. It was a gamble, but it came off. The Austrian venture speaks for itself.

Andrews: Great. You've been moving quality books – and in a new consumer group. So, what do you plan to do in Quebec?

Bender: Well, in the initial stages we're looking at the French-speaking market, because we have the product.

Andrews: But I assume you've given some thought to the English-speaking market.

Bender: Yes, but that's definitely our medium term aim. That's a tough nut to crack as you rightly suggested.

Andrews: So you intend to use Quebec as your launch pad, so to speak?

Bender: Launch pad, yes. Our ideal partner would be a chain which controlled outlets in English-speaking Canada and hopefully the United States as well. That way it would make it easier for us to broaden our base here at a later stage.

Callison: Well, how are you two progressing? She isn't giving you a hard time, is she Victor? Come on, sit down, bring me up to date ... Well, Victor?

Bender: Well, I think we're making progress. We are agreed that the North American market will not be an easy one, and we've been into the problems. Right?

Andrews: I'm still sceptical, but I think if we played up the unique features and played down the high price there's a good chance of success here. I think we should start by talking to the larger supermarket chains.

Bender: Fine, for your report, but I need a target date.

Callison: What can we do about that, Cecilia?

Andrews: What kind of ideas are we looking at here? First there's interviews with representatives of the retail food trade here in Quebec, a questionnaire, profiles of the major supermarket chains, and then I think you wanted to know if they have any prior experience with-er continuity promotions or part-work programmes, right?

Bender: Yes.

Callison: A complete feasibility study of your approach in Quebec.

Bender: That's right.

Andrews: I think we should stress the exclusivity angle. You wouldn't, I imagine, be offering the same titles to a competitor?

Bender: No, no, no, no, total exclusivity.

Callison: You should try and link the Austrian experience – show the similarities of the two markets, how it affects customer loyalty.

Andrews: Fine ...

Bender: We also need to find out how the supermarkets evaluate a programme.

Andrews: Of course. That's very important . . .

Callison: Tell you what, I'll get the exact terms of reference to you by the end of the week if that's all right?

Bender: Perfect. Now, we wanted to get moving with this as soon as possible – say within seven months at the latest – how does that fit in with your schedule?

Andrews: I don't see any real problems here, Mr Bender. We can get you an interview outline in ten days or so. Let's see, the surveys will take four weeks – which means I should be able to get you a full report in seven to eight weeks. Would that be OK?

Bender: Can we say seven weeks?

Andrews: OK. Seven weeks.

ROYCE-LYTTON FOODS

Scene 1: Outside a hotel in Kuwait

Anthony Newton: Well, Mr Rutherford? How are you getting on?

John Rutherford: I really don't know. I've spent all afternoon waiting for a phone call. Don't know what's going on. Can't get a commitment from anybody. I thought I might have had a deal tied up by now.

Newton: I wouldn't worry if I were you.

Rutherford: Oh, why not?

Newton: This is your first trip to the Middle East, isn't it?

Rutherford: Yes?

Newton: Things happen at a different pace round here. Have you met Sheikh Sayid yet?

Rutherford: Yes, I finally got to see him this morning.

Scene 2: Sheikh Sayid's office in Kuwait

Sheikh Sayid (after speaking for some time in Arabic on the phone): Mr Rutherford, this is a pleasure. How do you do?

Rutherford: Well, at last we meet. How do you do?

Sheikh Sayid: Please.

Rutherford: Thank you.

Sheikh Sayid: I hope you are enjoying your stay in Kuwait.

Rutherford: Oh yes. Although it's maybe a little longer than I had expected. It's very good of you to see me, Sheikh Sayid. As you know, what I'm ...

Sheikh Sayid: Where in England do you come from, Mr Rutherford?

Rutherford: The company is based at Hadleigh, in Suffolk. It's on the eastern side of England.

Sheikh Sayid: I know Sudbury very well. Magnificent countryside – Constable country?

Rutherford: Constable? Oh, yes. Yes. Well, anyway, our position is that we'd like to ...

Sheikh Sayid: Coffee?

Rutherford: Sorry? Oh, yes please. (The telephone rings.)

Sheikh Sayid: Excuse me for one moment, please. (Answers the phone in Arabic)

Rutherford (to servant): Oh, thank you.

Sheikh Sayid: Tell me about your company, Mr Rutherford.

Rutherford (to servant): No, No, I'm fine. Thanks.
(to Sheikh Sayid): The company? Well, Royce-Lytton handle all kinds of frozen poultry products.

Sheikh Sayid: Have you been in business long?

Rutherford: About fifteen years. We've been exporting to Europe for more than ten years and now we're looking for an opportunity to expand into ...

Sheikh Sayid: Fifteen years? Are you successful?

Rutherford: We've been very fortunate, the business has developed nicely.

Sheikh Sayid: I'm sure your success has been due to more than good fortune.

Rutherford: Well, we all put our shoulders to the wheel, er, work hard, that is.

Sheikh Sayid: Yes, I am aware of the expression. You know that we make many of our dishes from poultry? It is an important part of our diet.

Rutherford: Oh yes! We see it as an important market.

Sheikh Sayid: Well I can assure you it is. In fact there is an increasing demand throughout the Middle East for poultry of high quality, like yours.

Rutherford: Yes. That's exactly why I'm here. The point is ...

Scene 3: Outside the hotel

Newton: Well, I understand you might find it frustrating. People here don't like to rush straight into talking about deals and signing contracts.

Rutherford: It's hard work just staying on the subject.

Newton: I suppose you kept on trying to get back into it?

Rutherford: Why not? I didn't come all this way just for small talk. I'm sorry. I just don't know where I stand.

Newton: I expect things are moving.

Rutherford: I wish I could share your confidence.

Newton: As I said, there's no need to force the pace. When in Rome …

Rutherford: Do as the Romans do? I suppose you're right. Thank you, Mr Newton. Bye.

Newton: Bye-bye.

Scene 4: Sheikh Sayid' office

Sheikh Sayid: The Kuwait Trading Company has many interests in the Gulf – property, factories, shopping malls, hotels – the one you're staying in is owned by KTC.

Rutherford: That is very impressive. And you are also a major food importer?

(Abdullah Najibi enters and has a brief conversation with Sheikh Sayid in Arabic.)

Rutherford: Would you be interested in importing? Poultry products. Are you interested in importing any?

Sheikh Sayid: Mr Rutherford, we have arranged to move you into a special suite at the hotel. You will be more comfortable.

Rutherford: Oh you don't … only the room I had was all right – very comfortable … It's very kind of you.

Sheikh Sayid: We like to look after our important guests, Mr Rutherford.

Rutherford: Oh, I appreciate that. Well, it so happens we were hoping to clinch a deal of some kind in this area. We thought that KTC might be interested in . . . .

(The phone rings, Sheikh Sayid answers it and speaks in Arabic. When he has finished speaking, Rutherford continues.)

Rutherford: Would I be correct in thinking that KTC might be interested in a business venture with Royce-Lytton?

Sheikh Sayid: A hatchery and production facilities? Yes, in principle, I should think we might be.

Rutherford: Ah – I was thinking of something more along the lines of importing frozen products, to begin with.

Sheikh Sayid: Why think small when there are such excellent opportunities before us?

Rutherford: Well, to be honest, we don't know you, you don't know

us, not yet. We wouldn't want to jump the gun, eh?

Sheikh Sayid: You are very cautious, Mr Rutherford. This is an excellent quality in business. You know, we have foodstores all over the Arab world. We can start selling your poultry – tomorrow, if you are able to fulfil the usual conditions.

Rutherford: Conditions? What conditions were you thinking of?

Sheikh Sayid: All labelling in Arabic; the birds must be slaughtered according to Islamic laws – a certificate to that effect must be obtained from the Islamic Cultural Centre in London. I am sure you appreciate it's absolutely essential to us.

Rutherford: No problems on that score at all.

Sheikh Sayid: Good then. If that matter could be cleared out of the way, I think we might start to think about quantity.

(A servant arrives with coffee and halva)

Sheikh Sayid: Have you tried halva?

Rutherford: Ah, no … Mmm, very good.

Sheikh Sayid: Have some more.

Rutherford: I must admit I do have a bit of a sweet tooth.

Sheikh Sayid: Say six or seven thousand tons a year to begin with – maybe more. Chicken, that is.

Rutherford: Well, I, er … that's a lot of chicken.

Sheikh Sayid: Mr Rutherford, this is my general manager, Abdullah Najibi. He came to take us to a building site of a new villa. It is beautiful. You will like it. Shall we go?

JAUDEL FRANCE

Scene 1: Thomas Lang's office, New York

Keith Cooper: You read this?

Thomas Lang: So we've made it into the trade papers again, huh? They're saying we're on the rocks. First I've heard of it.

Cooper: You can bet Michèle Jeannot will have read it by now.

Lang: Oh come on Keith, I don't think Michèle's going to be too bothered about this. When she gets here, I want to be upbeat, Keith. Everything's under control, we're getting great results with Jaudel products, our business is going exactly where we want it to go. OK?

Cooper: We can't just shrug off what it says there.

Lang: We have to try and minimize it. Look, it might not even come

up. Butter her up a little bit, hm? I'm sure she'll come round to our way of seeing this.

Cooper: But Tom, it does put her in an advantageous position, if she wants to put pressure on us.

Lang: This is our annual sales meeting, that's all. We must keep it on that level. That article is speculative, but we have the facts and figures. Remember that, Keith.

Cooper: It all depends on how Madame Jeannot wants to interpret it, wouldn't you say?

(The phone rings.)

Lang: Tom Lang? Oh, good. Show her in, would you, please? Upbeat, Keith, remember.

Secretary: Madame Jeannot.

Lang: Hello Michèle. Lovely to see you in New York again.

Michele Jeannot: It's always a pleasure to be here, Tom.

Lang (to secretary): Hold all calls for the next hour, would you, please?

Secretary: Yes, Mr Lang.

Cooper: Hi Michèle, how was your flight?

Jeannot: Very pleasant – I came by Concorde. It's wonderful.

Cooper: Oh, good. Well, welcome back.

Lang: Won't you sit down? Well, er, let's get down to business, shall we? I've asked Keith to prepare a presentation of Rubens's distribution of Jaudel products over the last six years. I think that might be a good starting point, don't you Michèle?

Jeannot: By all means, Tom.

Lang: Keith? It's all yours.

Cooper: (commenting on slides): Thank you. Well, first, I'm pleased to report that once again, Jaudel products have done extremely well over here. In the folders in front of you, you'll find a complete breakdown of sales by product line and market. You'll notice that sales have increased 13% overall, from 3.8 million dollars to 4.3 million dollars. And our sales people report that demand continues to be strong. Our strongest markets are in the Northeast: Boston, New York, Philadelphia, and Washington DC. In fact this area accounts for 90% of our sales – the remaining 10% comes from our North Central markets – Chicago, Detroit and Cleveland.

Here we see our total sales revenue since year one. Sales have risen every year, from nine hundred and sixty-five thousand dollars in year one to over four million dollars at present, a fourfold increase. And

finally, our forecast of sales over the next five years …
I think you'll agree this is really impressive. Five years from now, we fully expect sales to reach nearly eight million dollars. Thank you.

Lang: Thank you Keith. Michèle?

Jeannot: A good clear picture … of sales in the Northeastern United States.

Lang: Well, Virtue Rubens sales in the rest of the US are negligible; the Northeast is our market.

Jeannot: Precisely, Tom, but frankly, we feel that the market for our products is much larger. I don't deny that Virtue Rubens has done a fine job with Jaudel in the Northeast, but we'd really like to see our products marketed throughout the US.

Lang: Seven years ago Jaudel wasn't even in this market. From zero to a four-million-dollar-a-year business in six years … now you can't …

Jeannot: I know, Tom, and I agree. I still say what about the rest of the country? We feel that it would be better to broaden our market base. The real growth for cosmetics is in the West and in the Sunbelt. That's where we should be looking now.

Lang: If you move into the Sunbelt, the costs will be astronomical! And you'll have little to show for it profit-wise.

Cooper: I really don't think you appreciate the problems of the American market, Michèle – the US is a number of regional markets, each quite different from the others. It's not easy to break into …

Jeannot: I didn't say it would be easy – it is simply necessary. As we see it, our US competition is fighting back hard. We cannot survive unless we develop our sales outside the Northeast.

Cooper: Michèle, do you realize how much it'd cost, what's involved? Transportation, distribution, advertising costs. It'd be crazy!

Lang: And don't forget any one of our regional markets is … well, at least the size of France!

Jeannot: We're aware of the costs, but what about the risks of not getting into these markets? Other French companies are moving up in the market place too. We have to stay ahead.

Lang (offering drink): Michèle?

Jeannot: Thanks.

Lang: I'm sure your suggestion would appear attractive to Jaudel, but believe me, we know the market. It won't work.

Jeannot: Are you trying to tell me that Virtue Rubens is unable to undertake a sales expansion in other areas?

Lang: It's more a question of investment and resources. We certainly couldn't dream of becoming involved with launching anything as big as you're suggesting.

Jeannot: I had our marketing people come up with a few figures for me. Their prediction isn't as enthusiastic as yours, Keith. They say that sales may be down by as much as half a million on your next year's prediction. They also tell me that growth could be substantially increased – by as much as 25% annually, if we sell in the West.

Lang: It's too risky. If we try and expand too quickly, it'll mean trouble.

Jeannot: You're talking about Virtue Rubens – of your problems in broadening your base!

Cooper: I'd like to see those figures, Michèle. You'll obviously have to prove that they're more accurate than mine.

Jeannot: I will, Keith. The thing is, gentlemen, I come here with a message from the President of Jaudel. He is anxious that Jaudel products should get nationwide markets in the US and to be perfectly frank, he suggests that if you are not prepared to … stick your neck out, he may have to consider an alternative distributor in North America.

Lang: Well that's clear enough. But I still maintain that to open up new markets in the Sunbelt and the West would lead to a long period of unprofitability. We're talking minuses here – for maybe up to five years. Virtue Rubens can't stand those kinds of long-term returns.

Jeannot: We must agree to disagree about that. I'll report all that you've said, but I feel that unless you can move towards our point of view, well, Jaudel may have to come to other arrangements.

MICROTRON ITALY

Scene 1: Richard Brewer's office, Houston, Texas

Richard Brewer: Yes, these look fine.

Leslie Reeves: Good.

Brewer: I was kind of hoping that he'd invite us out to San Diego to see this place of his …

Reeves: Sounds fantastic! Where exactly is it?

Brewer: It's along the beach there at San Clemente, right up on the hills overlooking the ocean.

Reeves: My idea of paradise!

John Hamilton: Could I have a quick word, Richard?

Brewer: What's on your mind, John?

Hamilton: You aren't really going to back one of these alternatives, are you?

Brewer: Now just hold on a minute, John. If you recall, I just wanted you to look the Baroncelli report over. Nothing's been decided yet.

Hamilton: Well, that's encouraging.

Reeves: Look John, you're not going to start in on that same old argument, are you? Al did a fine job with that report. Try supporting him, or at least keep an open mind!

Hamilton: Keep an open mind! I …

Brewer: Now, take it easy, please.

Hamilton: I'm sorry Richard, but more money goes into that subsidiary than any other in the entire group – and you know it, Leslie.

Reeves: And why? Because they're the most profitable, that's why. I just can't understand your problem.

Hamilton: I'll tell you my problem. As chief financial officer, I'm not prepared to commit that kind of money to an overseas division when the risks are so great!

Reeves: Risks? What risks, John? The European market is booming. We can hardly keep up with it.

Brewer: It's hardly a failing market, John.

Hamilton: Well, what about our other divisions? They're simply not getting their fair share of the corporate pie.

Brewer: OK John, I see your point. Why don't we get Baroncelli over here and discuss this with him? How does that sound?

Hamilton: Fine …

Brewer: He's bound to have given it some thought, and we can get it straight from the horse's mouth. (on phone) Get me Baroncelli, please.

Scene 2: Brewer's office

Brewer: Al's report shows that demand in Europe doubling over the next five years – to 54 million units. Now, if we get 12 per cent of that market, our sales'll more than double. Now, Microtron Italy's profits make up 50 per cent of our group's earnings from watches; so we obviously have to grow with that market. Now, the question is, how're we going to produce those extra units? Al, perhaps you could start?

Al Baroncelli: Thank you, Richard. Given our limited capacity in Brescia, I asked my people if they could come up with some way of satisfying this projected demand. They offered two solutions. The first is to expand capacity at our present location, but we'd soon find ourselves back where we started from since the space we have for expansion is limited, not enough capacity. The other idea is to take over another plant which is available nearby and renovate it, giving us two production units.

Hamilton: Al, these alternatives of yours: personally I don't see how we can justify either one of them, financially speaking. Now remember, you'll be reinvesting all your profits. Why don't you just run your facilities at capacity for a while?

Baroncelli: And lose out to our competitors? I can't accept that, John. I'm thinking about the future of Microtron Italia.

Reeves: I think, by and large, what Al is saying is there are sure signs of growth in Europe and we shouldn't just stand by and do nothing – I agree with him. I think ...

Hamilton: Do nothing? You have got to be kidding! I'm as bullish as anybody when it comes to investment! Why, I have personally ...

Brewer: Now let's settle down, please. As I see it, John's got a point: the Italian subsidiary has got a lot of help from us. Al, You've recently got the green light on new equipment and money to improve your production process ...

Hamilton: Which means that investment at our other plants has been minimal. Now we're talking about a further major investment here!

Reeves: John, why put so much money into Italy if you're not prepared to support it now? It doesn't make sense.

Baroncelli: OK, suppose we postpone any investment for two or three years maybe? What then? It'll cost just as much, maybe more, for the hardware then, but we'll have lost our place in the market. We've got to go for it now!

Brewer: There's got to be some middle ground here. John, supposing we said – just for a minute – that this expansion is necessary. How do we finance it?

Hamilton: Well, off the top of my head, Richard, there might be a way of, well, for instance, cutting back on some of our other expenses.

Baroncelli: Like what?

Hamilton: The digital watch division has the highest product development budget in the group – if we could find some way to reduce that outlay, maybe I could find a way to ...

Reeves: You've got to be crazy, John. Trade off future profits for short-term benefits?

Hamilton: I have the shareholders to think of.

Baroncelli: I couldn't accept that. And I bet the Board wouldn't agree to any cut-backs on key development work. It doesn't make business sense.

Hamilton: Well, neither does spending millions on one plant, when there are several other ideas in the works worthy of some consideration. Our Alabama site, for instance, could use the sort of investment being considered here – and start showing a profit.

Baroncelli: Surely the shareholders would appreciate their money being placed in the area of highest profit – look at the figures.

Hamilton: I know the figures Al. Nobody is suggesting that Brescia is dragging its feet in any way. But there are other considerations.

Reeves: Name one.

Hamilton: Well, currency fluctuations, for one: in Europe we get less for more, investment-wise.

Reeves: That loses meaning when it's compared to the potential growth and profits to be gained by expanding in Europe. I find it interesting that you mention the Alabama site ...

Hamilton: Oh, why?

Reeves: Alabama's your home state. Aren't you being a bit partial here? We all know how important the Alabama project is. But let's not lose sight of the group's overall objectives.

Hamilton: And what does that mean?

Brewer: Just a minute you two! Aren't we getting away from the subject? Now let's get back to the main issue ...

Baroncelli: That's fine with me. It's a simple matter of arithmetic.

Hamilton: Well, my 'arithmetic' tells me that a period of heavy investment in Brescia will only take cash away from other projects. It could jeopardise the profitability of the entire group.

Baroncelli: That would only be the case if we hit some snag or other.

Hamilton: Can you guarantee that we won't, Al?

Baroncelli: Of course not. Nobody could guarantee that kind of thing.

Brewer: Could I butt in here a second? Maybe, John, you could clear up a point for me? What exactly do you have in mind for the Alabama plant?

Reeves: Oh, he ...

Brewer: Now hold on Leslie. I think we should hear John's ideas.

Hamilton: Thank you, Richard. Well, the Alabama development guys have come up with a new product concept, and I believe in its viability. You've all seen the file on the Silex system?

Reeves: I see that as something for the late nineties, John. Long run, while we're talking about investment over the next three years here.

Hamilton: My feeling is that if we don't develop the Silex system now, our competitors will. Can you see us in ten years with a huge investment in Brescia producing obsolete watches? I say that we invest in the Alabama division, not in Europe.

Reeves: I think you're being totally unrealistic, and for reasons which I find – to be perfectly frank – biased. We're in business to make a profit. It's clear to me we should invest where the profit lies – Europe.

Baroncelli: Think of the shareholders.

Brewer: Well, we've got to come up with a recommendation for the board to consider. For my part I must say I can see good reasons for both ideas. The one sure thing is that we have to expand and we have to decide as to which way we're going to proceed.